# A
# PRISM
# ON
# GLOBALIZATION

## CORPORATE RESPONSES TO THE DOLLAR

SUBRAMANIAN RANGAN

*and*

ROBERT Z. LAWRENCE

BROOKINGS INSTITUTION PRESS
*Washington, D.C.*

*Copyright © 1999*
THE BROOKINGS INSTITUTION
*1775 Massachusetts Avenue, N.W., Washington, D.C. 20036*
*www.brookings.edu*

*Library of Congress Cataloging-in-Publication data*
Rangan, Subramanian.
    A prism on globalization : corporate responses to the dollar/
by Subramanian Rangan and Robert Z. Lawrence.
        p.    cm.
    Includes bibliographical references and index.

    ISBN 0-8157-7360-9 (alk. paper)
    ISBN 0-8157-7359-5 (pbk. : alk. paper)
    1. International business enterprises—Management. 2.
International business enterprises—United States—Management. 3.
Dollar, American. 4. Foreign exchange rates—United States. 5.
International economic integration. I. Lawrence, Robert Z., 1949—
II. Title.
    HD62 .4.R36 1999                                    99-6415
    658'.049–dc21                                          CIP


9 8 7 6 5 4 3 2 1
The paper used in this publication meets the minimum requirements of the American
National Standard for Information Sciences—Permanence of Paper for
Printed Library Materials, ANSI Z39.48-1984

Typeset in Palatino

Composition by Harlowe Typography
Cottage City, Maryland

Printed by R. R. Donnelley and Sons
Harrisonburg, Virginia

# ℔ THE BROOKINGS INSTITUTION

The Brookings Institution is an independent organization devoted to nonpartisan research, education, and publication in economics, government, foreign policy, and the social sciences generally. Its principal purposes are to aid in the development of sound public policies and to promote public understanding of issues of national importance.

The Institution was founded on December 8, 1927, to merge the activities of the Institute for Government Research, founded in 1916, the Institute of Economics, founded in 1922, and the Robert Brookings Graduate School of Economics and Government, founded in 1924.

The Board of Trustees is responsible for the general administration of the Institution, while the immediate direction of the policies, program, and staff is vested in the President, assisted by an advisory committee of the officers and staff. The by-laws of the Institution state: It is the function of the Trustees to make possible the conduct of scientific research, and publication, under the most favorable conditions, and to safeguard the independence of the research staff in pursuit of their studies and in the publication of the result of such studies. It is not a part of their function to determine, control, or influence the conduct of particular investigations or the conclusions reached.

The President bears final responsibility for the decision to publish a manuscript as a Brookings book. In reaching his judgment on competence, accuracy, and objectivity of each study, the President is advised by the director of the appropriate research program and weighs the views of a panel of expert outside readers who report to him in confidence on the quality of the work. Publication of a work signifies that it is deemed a competent treatment worthy of public consideration but does not imply endorsement of conclusions or recommendations.

The Institution maintains its position of neutrality on issues of public policy in order to safeguard the intellectual freedom of the staff. Hence interpretations or conclusions in Brookings publications should be understood to be solely those of the authors and should not be attributed to the Institution, to its trustees, officers, or other staff members, or to the organizations that support its research.

# *Foreword*

The phenomenon of globalization is frequently invoked to explain many features of our economy, yet the degree to which the world economy has in fact become truly integrated remains a matter of controversy. Some talk as if international integration is almost complete, while others believe that substantial barriers to the free flow of goods, services, and capital remain—that borders still matter. Likewise, multinationals are increasingly important participants in the global economy, yet the degree to which their presence transforms the behavior of international trade, investment, and production remains poorly understood. Does their presence make the world economy more or less responsive to international differences in costs? Are their pricing, sourcing, and investment responses radically different from those entailing arm's-length transactions?

In this study, Subramanian Rangan and Robert Lawrence attempt to answer these and other questions by examining the responses of U.S. multinationals to fluctuations in the dollar. They conclude that multinational enterprises are responsive to changes in international costs in both their pricing and sourcing decisions. Like their foreign counterparts, U.S. multinationals make their pricing decisions in light of local market conditions—they mark to market. In response to cost fluctuations, these firms also shift their sourcing faster and to a greater degree than domestic firms engaged in international trade. But these sourcing responses are also limited. Multinationals are less footloose than might be widely believed. Foreign affiliates become increasingly embedded in foreign economies the longer they are present there and the more technologically sophisticated the host country.

The authors use these findings to develop a more nuanced picture of the nature of globalization than is often drawn. They depict a world in which national boundaries remain important, not simply because of the formal obstacles represented by trade barriers and other policies, but also because national borders correlate sharply with information discontinuities that impede international exchange. Indeed, although foreign direct investment (FDI) and trade tend to operate as substitutes early on, in later stages that relationship turns more complementary. This, in the view of the authors, is because multinationalization helps firms bridge cross-border information discontinuities. Accordingly, they view multinationalization as a beneficial process and warn against government policies seeking to inhibit FDI.

The research for this book has been many years in the making. The authors wish to acknowledge numerous colleagues at Harvard and INSEAD who have helped in this work. Their greatest debt is to Raymond Vernon, F. M. Scherer, and Mun Ho, three individuals who gave guidance and feedback throughout the process. Ishtiaq Mahmood and, for the greater part of the project, Raghavendra Rau provided exceptional research assistance. They are grateful also to William Alterman, Jamil Baz, Terrence Burnham, Richard Cooper, Lorraine Eden, Dennis Encarnation, Antonio Fatas, Edward

"Monty" Graham, Jim Hines, Michael Knetter, Hans Peter Lenkes, Donald Lessard, Bjorn Lovas, Catherine Mann, Raymond Mataloni, Jeffrey Reuer, Shang-Jin Wei, and Srilata Zaheer for the help and guidance they gave us during one or another phase of the research. The authors also thank John Dunlop, Sidney Topol, and John White for help obtaining access to the firms and executives in our case studies. Rangan would also like to acknowledge Yves Doz, Gareth Dyas, Ludo van der Heyden, and INSEAD, without whose enthusiastic support this research would not have been possible. Our gratitude also goes to the Center for Business and Government at Harvard University, in particular to Roger Porter, the center director, and to Beverly Raimondo, the center's long-time (but now former) administrative director. Last but not least, we wish to thank Amy Christofer, Paula Holmes, and Susan Treffel for their friendly and able assistance over the long course of this research project.

At the Brookings Institution Press, Janet Walker was the managing editor and supervised this publication. Vicky Macintyre edited the manuscript, Carlotta Ribar proofread the pages, and Julia Petrakis provided the index. Research verifiers were Jennifer Eichberger and Takako Tsuji. The administrative assistant was Evelyn M. E. Taylor.

The project was generously funded by the Alfred P. Sloan Foundation.

The views expressed here are those of the authors and should not be ascribed to any of the persons whose assistance is acknowledged above, or to the trustees, officers, or other staff members of the Brookings Institution.

MICHAEL H. ARMACOST
*President*

*June 1999*
*Washington, D.C.*

# Contents

# A Borderless World and Nationless Firms? 1

O VER THE PAST fifty years the world economy has been shaped in large part by two mutually reinforcing developments. Technological innovations in communications and transportation have shrunk the distances that once separated the world's nations, and government policies have removed the barriers to trade and investment that segmented the world economy. Fueled by these developments, globalization has become the mantra of this era and the multinational enterprise (MNE) its priest.

In the 1950s U.S. firms stood almost alone at the global technological frontier. As obstacles to investment abroad declined and economies in the rest of the world recovered from the effects of World War II, American firms began discovering that their know-how and capital could be profitably deployed abroad. By the late 1970s U.S. multinationals had become a major factor in the global economy, accounting for almost 10 percent of the world's gross domestic product (GDP).[1] This foreign expansion of U.S. firms stabilized by the 1980s.[2]

As the prowess of firms headquartered in other nations grew, they, too, multinationalized and established and expanded their presence in the United States. This inward foreign direct investment into the United States shot up sharply during the latter half of the 1980s, ushering in a new era of economic interdependence.[3] Since then multinationals have played an increasing role in the economy in general, and in international trade in particular. In 1994, for example, more than 35 percent of U.S. exports and almost 43 percent of U.S. imports represented the intrafirm transactions of U.S.- and foreign-headquartered multinational enterprises.[4]

## Two Key Questions

Although such facts about "globalization" and "multinationalization" are clear, the significance of these interrelated developments remains controversial and raises some fundamental questions. Two such questions are the focus of this discussion. First, to what degree has the world economy become integrated? In other words, do borders still matter? And, second, how does the presence of multinational enterprises affect international economic behavior? That is to say, do multinationals matter?

### Do Borders Still Matter?

The first question revolves around the appropriate paradigm to apply to today's global economy. Should the traditional paradigm of a world economy divided into nation-states with national economies be replaced by a new paradigm of a borderless world?[5] In a world with separate national economies, the international responses of trade flows, capital, and the international diffusion of technology tend to be sluggish because of numerous obstacles. Some of these are created by policy barriers at borders (such as tariffs and quotas), which restrict trade, and barriers behind borders (such as regulations, national standards, competition policies, and government procurement), which may retard international competition. A second group arises from divergences in local culture, customs, tastes, language, and legal systems, all of which facilitate the segmentation of international markets. A third source is nature and geography, which raise the costs of transportation, communication, and information supply. Fourth are the collusive strategies of firms that are able to employ restrictive business practices, to inhibit competition from outsiders. Fifth are the advantages that accrue to local firms as first entrants, such as economies of scale, superior knowledge due to local learning by doing, and the development of specific consumer and national loyalties. To be sure, some of these constraints are present within purely domestic markets, but the existence of national boundaries makes their effects more powerful.

These obstacles give rise to national economies with distinctive consumers, producers, products, and competitive conditions. For one thing, international competition remains imperfect. Even where products are relatively similar, international price differences may persist because arbitrage is costly and difficult. Since international responses to shifts in relative costs are small and sluggish, governments enjoy considerable policy autonomy. Within a fairly broad range, they can implement domestic policies without adverse consequences, even when those policies reduce a region's international cost competitiveness. For the most part, domestic market conditions determine wages and profits. Firms—even those with foreign operations and affiliations—remain firmly embedded in their local economies. Their principal competitors are other domestic firms, and their pricing, marketing, and production behaviors are distinctively national in character. In such a world, firms and their national governments tend to think their interests are closely aligned.

But what would happen if the barriers separating national economies should disappear and capital and technology should become extremely mobile? Would these distinctive national attributes be eroded, and would national economies become close locational substitutes? In a world of this kind, small differences in policies and other measures that shift costs could have large effects on location and sourcing. "The law of one price" would prevail because (when measured in a common currency) the prices of internationally traded goods would be brought into line through arbitrage. This would also be a world of "factor price equalization" because international product prices would exert a strong influence on profits and wages in nations that produce similar products with similar technologies. More generally, the autonomy of national policy would be limited by international conditions.

In the absence of border barriers, competition would be global. Corporations would rapidly shift to locations that offered lower costs. Indeed, global competition would compel them to do so, because victory would go to the firms with the lowest costs, whereas firms mired in high-cost locations would eventually be driven out of business. In principle, then, knowing the extent to which the world economy remains nationally segmented or has become borderless is a crucial issue with important implications for both government and firm-level policy and behavior. The degree of policy autonomy, the conditions of competition in the markets for goods, and other factors could be radically different.

### Do Multinationals Matter?

As just noted, obstacles to international trade and investment can greatly influence economic behavior and outcomes. The next question to ask is what happens to economic behavior and patterns of outcomes when multinational firms take over a good deal of the international activity? How will trade, in particular, respond to changes in international costs and other conditions when multinationals are performing all the transactions? International economists often ignore multinational enterprises in their theoretical and empirical models. One case in point is the international adjustment process. Suppose a country is running a trade deficit that cannot be voluntarily financed because residents wish to import more from the rest of the world than they earn through exports. Two major adjustment processes will bring their spending into line: one operates via changes in the relative prices of domestic and international products, either directly or through changes in the exchange rate; the other is driven by changes in aggregate spending at home and abroad, which are in turn induced by changes in incomes and interest rates.

How would these adjustment processes be affected if multinational firms were significant participants in international commerce? Some speculate that multinationals would inhibit the adjustment process, because allocations within such firms would be less responsive to relative costs and prices than allocation within markets, and also because their allocation systems, behaving like typical hierarchies, would be less sensitive to costs than market systems, where prices are continuously available. Others believe that multinationals make little difference to the adjustment process. We think that multinational firms would be more responsive, in view of their global reach and surveillance capabilities.

Despite the possible implications of their activities, multinational companies have been by and large ignored in the economic models devised to explore the relationships between trade flows and relative prices and incomes. At the same time, a considerable literature has grown up around the question of how multinational firms behave. One view propounded there is that firms headquartered in particular nations display particular behavioral characteristics. The overseas affiliates of Japanese firms, for instance, are said to show considerable loyalty to suppliers from Japan and a great reluctance to source in foreign countries.[6] As for American exporters, they are considered myopic and likely to be swayed more by conditions in the United States than in the foreign markets in their export pricing policies. Such views clearly conflict with the traditional assumption of economics that firms from all nations are motivated to maximize profits and therefore should behave in a similar fashion when confronted with the same circumstances.[7]

The inescapable fact is that multinationals are becoming more significant participants in international trade and production, and hence their impact on economic behavior should be of concern to all those attempting to provide guidelines for public policy. If, on the one hand, the adjustment process is becoming less responsive as a result of the activity of multinationals, the size of the relative price changes required to achieve any given amount of adjustment may have to be correspondingly larger. But such action could cause real exchange rate changes to become volatile.[8] At the same time, it could mitigate some of the dislocation that any given price changes might cause. On the other hand, if the process is becoming increasingly sensitive to cost differentials, so that not only the flow of goods but entire plants tend to shift in response to cost differences, then the adjustment process might be facilitated, although the dislocation caused by policies and other variables that tend to affect relative costs would become increasingly greater.

From various analyses of multinational behavior, it appears that firms with operations in several countries are both willing and able to switch the location of their production in response to changes in cost differentials. As a consequence, the impact of the multinationals is the cause of growing concern even beyond the adjustment process. Some fear that "runaway plants" in the United States and "delocalization" in France will cause a serious loss of jobs. Others complain that shifting production abroad will weaken labor's bargaining power. Some also wonder whether the nation-state will be able to tax capital. If multinational location decisions are extremely responsive to cost differences, any attempt to increase corporate taxes will be met with outflows of capital, and it will become extremely difficult to redistribute from capital to labor. Furthermore, efforts at social regulation that are redistributive in character will discourage international investment and ultimately be paid for by immobile factors: labor and farmers.

Another possibility is that once they enter a domestic economy, multinationals may actually become increasingly embedded in it. In that case, there would probably be no large responses to small price changes. If anything, firms may shift sluggishly, once they have sunk substantial resources into domestic production facilities. Paradoxically, under these circumstances the rise of multinationals may help restore the autonomy of domestic policy and reduce some of the effects of globalization. In short, the implications of multinationals' behavior for both adjustment and globalization can no longer be ignored.

## How to Approach Multinationals

The questions posed here are best explored by examining the responses of multinationals to the unprecedented shifts in the U.S. dollar that started during the late 1970s and continued through the 1980s. The exercise may be broken down into several steps. As chapter 2 discusses, the first is to determine how multinationals price their products and thus whether borders still matter. If borders no longer matter, prices should experience similar changes in all markets. By contrast, if border effects remain significant, firms will be able to "price to market," that is, to set prices in response to unique domestic conditions. The next step, outlined in chapter 3, is to look at the cost shifts resulting from exchange rate changes and assess the extent to which multinationals' sourcing and production decisions are sensitive to these cost changes and whether firms headquartered in different nations respond differently. The last step, discussed in chapter 4, is to compare the responses of multinational trade with that of arm's-length trade.

The findings presented in these chapters are primarily the result of an econometric analysis, although the discussion also draws on some surveys and case studies. This approach was taken in part to ensure that changes with important but not fully visible implications for the international economy are not overlooked. Such changes may occur in a variety of circumstances. Suppose that components imported from the United States represent a small share of the overall value of sales by U.S. multinationals in Europe, say, 10 percent, while 90 percent of their value added comes from a local source. If the share sourced locally were to drop slightly, from 90 to 89 percent, the change might not appear significant for the firm, but from the viewpoint of the United States, this could represent an increase in export sales of 10 percent, which could be highly significant. Qualitative surveys that ask executives if they are highly responsive to the exchange rate might give a completely different impression.

Another point to mention at the outset is that this study is based almost entirely on data from the United States and on the behavior of U.S. and foreign firms there. These are the most comprehensive and readily available data, but the conclusions drawn from them would obviously be more convincing if validated with other sets of data and samples.

Note, too, that for convenience we have drawn a rather sharp distinction between intra- and extrafirm trade, and between the behavior of firms and the behavior of markets. We are well aware, however, of the variety of intermediate relationships between and among buyers and sellers that help economize on transaction costs and mitigate market failures and what we have termed discontinuities. In an international context these include licensing, joint ventures, alliances, and franchising. All are likely to increase as globalization continues.

## The Findings

Our first finding is that U.S. multinationals price to market: U.S.-owned firms abroad subject their American-based costs to a markup that reflects local demand conditions. Traditional macro-economic studies based on conventional export price equations come to a quite different conclusion, which is that U.S. exporters, unlike exporters from other major economies, fully pass through changes in their U.S. costs into their export prices. We believe that such studies have mistakenly relied on export price data, which to a great extent reflect the price at which U.S. multinational firms transfer goods to their foreign subsidiaries, rather than the price that multinationals charge to their final customers. In ignoring the role of multinationals, the price elasticity estimates obtained using aggregate trade volumes and prices conflate three different response channels: sales of (extrafirm) exports, responding to changes in export prices; multinational (foreign affiliate) sourcing decisions, responding to changes in U.S. costs; and the U.S. component of multinational final sales, responding to changes in over-all volumes of sales induced by changes in costs.

U.S. multinationals respond to changes in international relative costs in both their pricing and their sourcing decisions. Where exports are concerned, however, any shifts in volume following such cost changes reflect internal sourcing decisions rather than shifts in total sales volumes. In other words, the decision hinges on the substitutability of inputs from the United States and other countries, rather than the substitutability of the products of U.S. foreign affiliates with those of their foreign competitors.

Since the internal sourcing elasticity is similar in magnitude (that is, about 1½) to the final demand elasticity obtained for exports, it turns out that the specification used by conventional modelers actually performs reasonably well in prediction. But if this response were different, ignoring these distinctive channels could be a costly forecasting mistake. Moreover, by interpreting the pricing behavior as a complete pass-through into final prices, researchers could erroneously conclude, first, that U.S. managers are basically different, or that nationality matters; and, second, that U.S. firms are unable to price to market either because these markets are so open that market segmentation is impossible or because U.S. firms have no pricing power.

Since price data are not available for the final sales of U.S. multinationals, we use the novel approach of inferring pricing behavior from price-cost margins. Our conclusion that U.S. firms do price to market suggests that globalization has actually not eliminated the ability of firms to price-discriminate. This suggests that they retain residual pricing power and that markets are sufficiently segmented to prevent arbitrage.

If treated with caution, the price-cost margins that we generate can also be used to measure the degree of competition faced by U.S. multinationals. In theory, these margins would be expected to decline over time in an increasingly competitive world economy. In fact, these margins declined substantially between the 1960s and 1970s—when firms from other developed countries converged to U.S. technological levels and in response U.S. firms reduced the pricing premiums they once enjoyed—but since then the process does not appear to have continued. This suggests that the international maturation of U.S. multinationals was already fairly advanced by the mid-1970s.

The fact that firms from many countries do price to market implies that exchange rate changes are not always fully passed through into the prices paid by consumers. This serves to reduce some of the demand-side responses in the adjustment process, but it also means that exchange rates lead to shifts in profitability, which in turn eventually lead to adjustment on the supply side, but over longer periods of time.

Our second finding, as explained in chapter 3, is that the international sourcing decisions of U.S. multinationals do reflect international relative costs. But they are also related to a nation's underlying technological capabilities and to the length of time that multinationals have been present in the domestic economy. Indeed, multinationals are far more local than one might suspect. At least in developed countries, the source of about 90 percent of the value of their final sales usually resides in the local economy. This is true both for the foreign affiliates of U.S. firms in developed countries and for the U.S. affiliates of firms headquartered outside the United States. In developing countries the share that local sources contribute to final value is much smaller, although the longer that multinationals stay in the country, the higher this percentage is likely to be. This supports the notion that multinationals are not distinct enclaves. Although they might transfer know-how and certain key inputs internationally, over time they become deeply embedded in the local economy. Even in the case of Japanese multinationals in the United States, which used to source a high share of value added from Japan, this practice ceased in the 1990s. The earlier high Japanese share therefore probably reflected the recent vintage of the investment and the strong dollar rather than its national origins.

The degree to which multinationals add value locally is also a function of the capabilities of the country in which they operate. The more advanced the country, the higher the share of value added locally. Cheap labor is therefore not the preponderant determinant of investment by these firms, although there may be some labor-intensive industries and firms for which this is the case. In other words, the less developed the country, the higher the share of value added produced in the United States.

Our third finding is that the responses of intrafirm trade to exchange rate changes are both more rapid and larger than those of extrafirm trade. This result suggests that search, deliberation, and other transaction costs play a crucial role in the international adjustment process, and that multinational firms enjoy particular advantages there. The different lag structures for income and price effects indicate a qualitative difference between actions that are replicative and those that require search, deliberation, and adjustment. When demand increases, the firm must simply increase the scale of its behavior. Its major concern is sufficient capacity. To be sure, such adjustment could take time if capacity has to be built, but there will be little uncertainty associated with how to expand. When demand falls, the response is even more straightforward. It may be painful to reduce production, but there are no serious questions about how it should be done. By contrast, when prices change, the firm may have to change its behavior: it may have to search to find new suppliers; appraise which of several suppliers is most suitable; determine whether suppliers will be reliable and compatible with the rest of its operations; and change product designs and production to make use of the new supplies. All of these decisions will take time, and because of the risks and uncertainty associated with them, adjustment is likely to be gradual and to take place in stages. New suppliers might be given some trial orders and evaluated until sufficient experience is built up. It should therefore come as no surprise that the adjustment to price changes will take longer than adjustment to income changes.

As just mentioned, multinational firms appear to have certain advantages when the adjustments are on the international plane. Their extensive relationships, in particular, facilitate search and deliberation and reduce adjustment risks. Accordingly, they might be expected to adjust more rapidly, particularly in response to price changes. By contrast, progressive and gradual switching is more typical of arm's-length responses.

## Implications of the Findings

What do our results suggest about the nature of the global economy, the future of intrafirm trade, and the role of government policy?

### *A Borderless World?*

Clearly, national borders still matter: they continue to engender and coincide with important *discontinuities* stemming from government policy, geography, and societal differences. In addition, we would emphasize the role of information discontinuities, which create search and deliberation problems for trading and manufacturing firms. Search problems—the difficulties in identifying suitable exchange partners—are likely to play a key role in the lagged responses to exchange rate changes. Both search and deliberation problems may account in large part for the small price elasticities in trade, and, more broadly, for the "home bias" observed in international trade and finance. The information discontinuity view of national borders also helps explain why firms can price to market and why trade responses to income changes are faster (and larger) than responses to relative price changes.

Contrary to the impression created by frenzied movements in world currency markets and short-term capital flows, a large part of the global economy is actually characterized by visible stickiness and considerable lags in adjustment.[9] This accords with the mounting empirical evidence in international trade and finance, which indicates that national borders continue to matter far more than more naïve models might imply.[10] Even when exchange rate changes cause large and "permanent" shifts in relative prices, the geographic distribution of economic activity shifts slowly and hesitatingly.[11] Established buyer-supplier relationships appear sticky, and switching takes place with considerable lags. This does not mean, however, that at the margin both extra- and intrafirm trade and sourcing are unresponsive to shifts in income or in relative costs.

If anything, our results suggest that the two contrasting paradigms of national economies and a borderless world are incomplete and capture only part of a more complex and subtle story. The ability to exploit global markets by sourcing inputs and capital from the lowest cost locations is certainly an important part of the competitive picture. But it is only part of the story. Other competitive advantages accrue from locating close to key suppliers and from proximity to the market. These latter benefits are not easily abandoned, even in the face of substantial changes in costs.[12]

Our results also suggest that foreign direct investment (FDI) helps multinational firms bridge cross-border discontinuities. After controlling for firm size, industry, and partner country, we find that U.S. multinationals are able to respond faster and more vigorously to common exchange rate changes than most domestic U.S. firms in the same industry. Although formal border barriers, currencies, customs regulations, and the like represent obstacles for both intra- and extrafirm trade, eliminating them does not fully remove the greater transaction costs arising from differences in language, culture and behavior, or legal systems. And although the costs of gathering information about product availability and price can be reduced by revolutionary innovations such as the Internet, gaps in information concerning quality, reliability, compatibility, and trust still bedevil the deliberation process. These are all areas in which multinationals with foreign facilities are likely to have an advantage. Even the routine operation of those facilities generates a set of business relationships, a continually replenished stock of information about actual prices, and detailed knowledge about the existence, location, and precise needs and capabilities of buyers and suppliers in that region. Hence the multinational enterprise is conferred with privileged access to valuable information and connections in multiple currency areas.[13] Indeed, we can reject the view that multinationals are an impediment to trade and that intrafirm international trade is stickier than arm's-length trade, or that they are footloose entities.

### The Future

A striking feature of the postwar period is that trade has grown more rapidly than incomes. Although this trend must subside when all output is traded, it is likely to continue for the foreseeable future. Also, the erosion of discontinuities inherent in globalization is likely to continue. All the same, locations and geography will not cease to matter. After all, it is unlikely that information discontinuities (particularly those relevant to deliberation) will be completely eliminated. In addition, as market competition intensifies, specialization will become increasingly necessary. Indeed in many product areas, instead of the homogenization predicted by numerous observers of globalization, differentiation is likely to result. Even without borders, local economies could develop distinctive advantages that would provide their policymakers with some autonomy.

Put succinctly, there is good reason to believe that the "home bias" will be less marked over the next decades, but it will not disappear in our macro patterns. Distance will still continue to play a disproportionately larger role in international exchange than that suggested by the associated costs of transportation and telecommunication.

*Market versus Intrafirm Trade*

As border barriers and discontinuities continue to shrink, both intra- and extrafirm international trade will increase, but it is unclear which of these will grow faster. Non-U.S. multinationals expanded their economic activity considerably between 1985 and 1995, and their international, intrafirm shipments will in all likelihood become even more important in world trade. But the U.S. experience—especially the lack of change in intrafirm trade as a share of total U.S. trade between 1985 and 1994 (see table 1-1)—suggests that this growth may plateau.

Although multinationalization has expanded intrafirm international trade, another powerful trend, "marketization," has been helping to reduce it. More and more large firms are downsizing, performing only their core activities in-house and all other activities outside the firm. This development is being abetted in part by heightened competition, which may reduce the edge firms have in certain activities and force them to go outside to regain it. Technological innovations also induce outsourcing, particularly through reduced search costs. With the Internet, for example, buyers and sellers can find one another far more easily and cheaply than ever before. This allows smaller and more distant suppliers to find customers that were too expensive to locate in the past. And buyers are more likely to find products that are matched to their needs.

Globalization has also brought increased variety. As Adam Smith taught, the larger the market, the greater the potential for specialization. An expanding market provides a wider array of differentiated products, which are more likely to meet the needs of producers, who will therefore prefer external purchases. A market that offers greater choice and reliability also increases the advantage of sourcing flexibility, particularly for components that are more or less standardized.

**Table 1-1.** *Intrafirm Shares in U.S. Manufacturing Exports Accounted for by U.S. and Foreign Multinational Enterprises, 1966–94*[a]

Percent unless stated otherwise

| Exports | 1966 | 1977 | 1985 | 1989[b] | 1994[b] |
|---|---|---|---|---|---|
| | | | *Year* | | |
| *U.S. manufacturing exports* | | | | | |
| Total value in millions of current dollars | 22,088 | 91,946 | 164,381 | 272,260 | 435,991 |
| Total | 100.0 | 100.0 | 100.0 | 100.0 | 100.0 |
| Shipped by U.S. parents in manufacturing | 62.0 | 73.4 | 72.1 | 62.8 | 56.2 |
| To their majority-owned foreign affiliates | 24.2 | 28.0 | 32.3 | 29.0 | 26.5 |
| Shipped by U.S. parents in wholesale trade | 6.4 | 10.9 | 12.1 | 5.8 | 5.5 |
| To their majority-owned foreign affiliates | 0.9 | 0.7 | 0.5 | 0.6 | 0.8 |
| Shipped by U.S. manufacturing affiliates of foreign parents | n.a. | 3.9 | 7.8 | 11.7 | 11.1 |
| To their parents and affiliates | n.a. | 1.5 | 2.2 | 4.9 | 5.4 |
| Shipped by U.S. wholesale trade affiliates of foreign parents | n.a. | 3.1 | 4.0 | 6.8 | 7.1 |
| To their parents and affiliates | n.a. | 1.9 | 2.3 | 4.6 | 4.9 |
| Shipped by other U.S. entities | n.a. | 8.7 | 4.0 | 12.8 | 20.1 |
| Total intrafirm share in U.S. manufacturing exports excluding petroleum and coal products | 25.1 | 32.1 | 37.3 | 39.1 | 37.6 |

Source: Authors' estimates based on data from U.S. Department of Commerce, *Statistical Abstract of the United States, 1971, 1995; Trade and Employment*, various issues; U.S. Department of Commerce, Bureau of Economic Analysis, *U.S. Direct Investment Abroad* (henceforth USDIA), various issues; *Foreign Direct Investment in the U.S.*, various issues.

a. Excluding petroleum and coal products.

b. U.S. exports by U.S. parents in 1989 and 1994 have been adjusted down to avoid double-counting of exports made by U.S. affiliates of foreign parents.

n.a. Not available.

Another critical factor in today's markets is the reduced cost of pricing. Current information technology makes it cheaper to attach prices to commodities and contingencies. Whereas the need to reduce risk through diversification once drove firms to form conglomerates, today a dazzling range of markets for securities and derivatives makes it possible to reduce risk through markets rather than through firms. Although the large corporate groups operating in many countries indicate the advantages of internal intragroup allocation of capital when financial markets are underdeveloped, more and more small firms are raising capital externally. To be sure, the pressures for more precise pricing come from increased competition (owing to changes in policy such as deregulation and the reduction in trade barriers), but the role played by technology in facilitating these changes should not be underestimated.

An equally important force is the pace of change in technologically dynamic areas. In slow-moving industries, firms can innovate internally, but if they need to produce complex products containing a wide range of ever-changing components, there is a clear advantage to outsourcing components and services in which the firm is not a leader. Smaller firms with narrowly focused R&D efforts may then step in to fill this role.

The new information technology is also making manufacturing systems more flexible. A major driving force in the industrial revolution was the achievement of scale economies through the production of standardized products in large plants. Information technology on the plant floor not only increases product variety but permits smaller firms to produce at efficient levels, thereby making, in many settings, plant or product scale less important.

Yet another benefit of technology is that it reduces the need for proximity. Instantaneous and inexpensive communication and transportation make it more possible to take advantage of alternative sourcing possibilities, both domestically and internationally. Suppose that labor in a particular area is too expensive to undertake data processing there. With modern technology, the work can easily be done in distant locations, either in a firm's own plants or in foreign plants.

In sum, with greater policy liberalization, capability convergence among firms in different nations, and advances and specialization in technology, two developments are taking place: (1) firms are becoming increasingly multinational, and in the process stimulating a growth in intrafirm trade; (2) the (international) market is becoming more attractive, and the role of extrafirm trade is growing as well. In the case of the United States, these trends appear to have increased at relatively similar speeds over the past two decades. It is hard to predict whether this relationship will change in the future.

*Policy*

In much of the world, the current trade policy agenda rests on the assumption that border and nonborder policies continue to inhibit international integration. Therefore its aim is to reach new international agreements that reconcile different national policies so that the benefits of international integration can be more fully realized. This is the reason for the push for new rules for standards, foreign investment, and competition policy in multilateral forums such as the World Trade Organization (WTO) and the Organization for Economic Cooperation and Development (OECD) and in regional settings such as the European Union and Asia-Pacific Economic Cooperation (APEC). If markets are already highly integrated, however, then the potential benefits of additional integration may not be large. Since these agreements are often surrounded by controversy, it may not be worthwhile to expend the political capital that may be required to achieve them. Indeed, according to some observers, "globalization may have gone too far," and it may be necessary to take steps to restore a greater degree of national autonomy.[14]

This study provides support for continued efforts to enhance the contestability of international markets through international agreements on investment and competition policies. The evidence that multinational firms can price to market suggests that international competition remains less than perfect and that international markets continue to be segmented.

Policies that would liberalize international investment will also find support here. Although the case for free trade has been widely accepted, the case for free direct foreign investment is still being debated.[15] Some who favor import liberalization continue to advocate restrictions or conditions on foreign direct investment. In the view put forward here, such conditions could reduce the benefits from international integration. When an innovation occurs, there will be gains to producers who can realize profits and to consumers who can obtain products that are superior to or cheaper than those they can obtain elsewhere. The conventional method for exploiting these opportunities, when producers and consumers are located in different countries, is the arm's-length transaction that occurs through trade in the international marketplace. In many circumstances, however, the market may not be the most efficient mechanism for such transactions. Markets work well when contracts can be written cheaply, products specified precisely, and prices easily provided. These properties will lead firms to deal at arm's length. But when these attributes are absent, markets are less effective.

Even if know-how is best developed in a particular market, it may still be best exploited close to the ultimate buyer, or at a location in which production costs are cheaper. Although licensing such know-how is certainly an option, for various familiar reasons it will at times be impractical or too costly to do so. In such cases, efficiency is best served by international transfers within the firm. Countries that deny themselves access to foreign investment reduce not only the returns to such innovations abroad, but also their own opportunities to benefit from such innovations. They will lose the textured flows of information and knowledge that can be channeled within firms. Either they will never gain access to such innovations, or they will do so at a higher cost.

Concern about the behavior of multinationals has led some observers to advocate control of foreign direct investment.[16] These firms, they fear, will remain enclaves and fail to transfer their key technologies to the local economy. Or they will tend to be footloose and less loyal than local firms in response to unfavorable developments. They may even stifle the international adjustment process. Our findings suggest these concerns may be misplaced: if countries offer attractive conditions for production, most multinationals will respond with increased domestic value added. Multinationals have strong reasons to retain a local presence, and their ability to respond to and evade local taxes and other redistributive measures will be limited. To reiterate, over time they will become increasingly embedded in the local economy. Furthermore, their behavior appears to be driven more by rational profit-maximizing goals than by nationalistic considerations.

A considerable body of econometric evidence indicates that price elasticities in international trade are low, between 1 and 2. This implies that fairly large changes in relative international prices may be required to effect large transfers of savings internationally. Whether it is more efficacious to effect international transfers of savings through changes in the nominal exchange rate or in domestic prices remains a controversial issue that is beyond the scope of this study.[17] For our purposes, it suffices to say that multinationals do not impede the process. Other things being equal, their responses appear more sensitive to cost changes than those of market transactions between unrelated parties.

# Pricing Responses of U.S. Multinationals | 2

I N THE MID-1980s, when the dollar declined from its record highs, observers impatiently waited for the U.S. trade balance to respond. Instead of improving, the deficit continued to worsen in the short run, and this sparked considerable economic research of both an empirical and theoretical nature. The empirical research suggested that important differences in the behavior of U.S. and foreign firms helped account for the sluggish response. American exporters, it appeared, fixed their prices in dollar terms and fully passed the exchange rate effects through into their foreign currency prices. Indeed, between 1985 and 1989 the U.S. export price index compiled by the Bureau of Labor Statistics (BLS) moved precisely in line with the *domestic* wholesale prices (see figure 2-1).[1] This implied that, measured in dollars, any rise in U.S. export values rested heavily on the demand responses of foreign buyers, a response that history suggested could take time.[2]

Foreign producers selling in the United States, however, appeared to behave differently. In particular, Japanese and German

**Figure 2-1.** *U.S. Export and Domestic Prices, 1980–90*[a]

Index, 1980 = 100

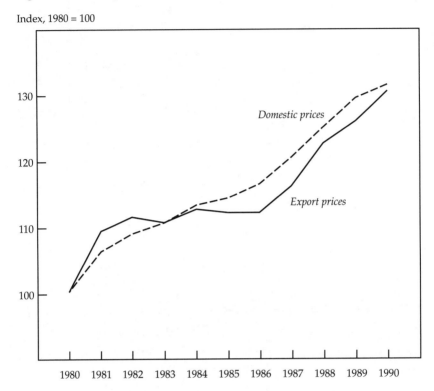

Source: Lawrence, "U.S. Current Account Adjustment," table 5, p. 354.
a. Prices were constructed by the authors and exclude agricultural and computer products. For details of how these indexes were constructed, see Lawrence, "U.S. Current Account Adjustment," pp. 351–53.

firms competing in U.S. markets stabilized their dollar prices and allowed their profit margins to shrink, apparently in an attempt to maintain U.S. market share. Although this behavior helped dampen the *J*-curve effect that comes from higher import prices, it was thought to be stifling the adjustment process.[3]

With the passage of time and further research, these misgivings about the trade adjustment process were shown to be misplaced.[4] The response of trade flows to the dollar was both substantial and predictable from traditional econometric specifications, but it took far longer than many observers had anticipated. Nonetheless, the debate about U.S. adjustment stimulated important theoretical research. Theory predicts full pass-through when firms set prices by applying constant markups over marginal cost. However, the phenomenon of incomplete pass-through, termed "pricing to market," also received considerable attention.[5] Pricing to market refers to the behavior of exporters, who, in an attempt to maintain their foreign currency prices at an optimal level, absorb at least some portion of changes in the exchange rate in their profit margins. In general, they will let profit margins rise when the exchange rate depreciates and fall when the exchange rate appreciates.[6] What is important, changes in the foreign market prices of these firms will deviate from changes in their home country prices in a direction that is sensitive to local market conditions and the prices offered by competitors.[7]

Why firms with the requisite market power might not fully pass through exchange rate changes into prices has been attributed to various factors: the role of market share and demand dynamics; sunk costs, supply-side dynamics, and hysteresis; the long-term value maximizing the strategic behavior of firms in *oligopolistic* markets; and the defensive responses of firms to temporary "misalignments" of exchange rates.[8] But the very plausibility of these theoretical demonstrations of the optimality of pricing-to-market behavior raises an important question. Why was the behavior of American firms apparently so different from that of their foreign counterparts? Why did they not exploit the opportunity offered by the decline in the U.S. dollar? It has been suggested that firms competing in oligopolistic markets, where market shares matter and where reentry (sunk) costs are high, would, at least in the short run, tend to cushion local currency prices from fully reflecting changes in the exchange rate. Yet, although American manufactured exports are heavily concentrated in precisely those product areas in which oligopolistic pricing practices ought to dominate, U.S. exporters appeared almost mechanically to pass exchange rate changes through into their export prices.

## Reasons for the U.S. Pricing Behavior

The pass-through behavior of U.S. firms has been attributed to four factors: myopia, menu costs, arbitrage, and data problems.

### Myopia

American managers, some researchers argue, are inward looking and simply do not care about foreign sales; their pricing behavior reflects a "take it or leave it" attitude. But this view is hard to square with the strong interest in foreign markets that U.S. firms have shown in their direct foreign investment behavior. Moreover, most economists would be reluctant to ascribe behavioral differences to national character traits that are not based on economic factors. An alternative explanation (which applies only to responses to dollar appreciation) is "short-termism." That is to say, U.S. firms have high discount rates and thus are unwilling to see their profit margins erode.[9] But this view does not explain why U.S. firms did not raise their profit margins when the dollar declined.

### Menu Costs

Others maintain that American firms do not price-discriminate across markets because such policies are too costly to administer. After all, exports account for only a small portion of overall sales.[10] Indeed, the *Fortune* list of the fifty largest U.S. exporters in 1990 shows only eleven firms for whom exports exceed 20 percent of sales. Apparently the supply curve for U.S. exports measured in dollars is infinitely elastic in the relevant range. But this explanation also appears to be implausible. Firms should behave optimally on *all* their sales. The relevant issue is not whether exports are small compared with domestic sales, but whether they are sufficiently large to justify the additional cost of administering strategic pricing policies. Since U.S. exports of manufactured goods are concentrated among a few large firms and in the aggregate actually exceed those of Japan in dollar value, this argument surely does not withstand scrutiny.

### Arbitrage

Another view is that pricing to market implies a divergence in *changes* in a firm's prices internationally and thus an ability to segment markets without fear of arbitrage. U.S. firms, proponents of this view argue, face a higher degree of pressure from arbitrageurs (than do their Japanese or German counterparts) and are therefore less able—or perhaps even unable—to price-discriminate across markets.[11] But arbitrage possibilities should surely run in both directions. If the United States is so open that Americans cannot price-discriminate abroad (so that price deviations between, say, the United States and Germany for American products will be arbitraged away), why does the process not work in reverse for German goods sold in the United States? In fact, within-industry behavior has been found to be similar for U.S., German, and Japanese firms.[12]

### Data Problems

Yet another explanation is that the price data on which these findings are based are themselves questionable.[13] The BLS, it is pointed out, collects data on both domestic and export prices through mail surveys, which in many responding companies are answered by the same department. Some firms have reportedly been reluctant to provide different export and domestic prices for the same products, for fear of being accused of price discrimination.[14] We believe that this argument has some merit and should be taken more seriously than it has been up to now.[15]

In an effort to get to the bottom of this controversy, we decided to violate the norms of our profession by actually asking firms what they do. We appended a set of questions on pricing behavior to a survey of the exchange rate responses of twenty-five major U.S. companies conducted by Donald Lessard and Srilata Zaheer of the Massachusetts Institute of Technology.[16] In addition, we interviewed senior executives responsible for pricing in three major U.S. exporting firms. Our surveys concentrated on the behavior of firms in the face of the massive depreciation of the dollar after 1985. The responses pointed to something more like the pricing-to-market behavior one might expect in theory than the complete pass-through behavior reflected in the BLS export price index: that is to say, 80 percent of the firms surveyed said their pricing decisions were made in the local market, and between half and two-thirds indicated they had "maintained their local prices" in the face of the precipitous decline of the dollar between 1985 and 1989.[17]

What, then, is one to make of the discrepancy between the empirical findings that exchange rates are almost fully passed through into export prices and the theoretical supposition (and evidence from surveys and case studies) that U.S. firms price to market? The key to resolving this apparent contradiction lies in recognizing that, in an important number of cases, official U.S. export prices do not actually indicate the prices paid by *final purchasers* of American products abroad. For a significant proportion of U.S. exports, particularly those that take the form of intrafirm trade, export price changes are more likely to reflect changes in the internal prices at which products are transferred between headquarters and their affiliates. Moreover, export prices will reflect transfer prices not only for most of the approximately 40 percent of manufactured exports that are shipped overseas intrafirm, but also, because of sampling practices, for a significant percentage of the 40 percent of manufactured exports that are exported at arm's length by U.S. multinationals.[18]

As this chapter shows, support for this interpretation can be found in the pricing behavior of U.S. multinationals following the exchange rate changes of the 1980s, particularly the dollar depreciation after 1985. As theory would predict, U.S. multinationals located abroad do *not* fully pass through exchange rate changes into their final product prices, and they alter their margins in a manner consistent with pricing-to-market behavior. Hence it is misleading to use the BLS export price index as a proxy for final purchase prices.[19] Another important point, explored more fully in chapter 3, is that the sourcing decisions of U.S. multinationals are responsive to changes in relative costs. Since export prices (and wholesale prices) provide reasonable proxies for these costs, economists who have used these series in explaining trade flows have actually been (almost) right, albeit for the wrong reasons.

## The BLS Export Price Index and Intrafirm Trade

In principle, it would not be surprising to see a multinational enterprise pricing exports differently for internal distribution and external sales. When pricing its product, a discriminating monopolist will, in theory, differentiate the markup over marginal cost according to demand conditions in different market segments (see the theoretical models of international pricing in appendix A). But if a firm can source its product from a variety of locations, it should ensure that the marginal cost of sourcing from each location is equalized. This suggests that both sourcing and pricing decisions require measures of marginal cost, and that such information should be widely known by and be fairly transparent to the decisionmakers. However, sales prices to customers would differ in response to local market conditions.[20]

Firms could implement their strategies on a centralized or decentralized basis: corporate headquarters could dictate all pricing and sourcing decisions, or the firm could rely on a decentralized internal market in which intermediate products are made available to various subsidiaries at a price that reflects marginal costs. In the latter case, the subsidiaries would make independent pricing decisions in their sales (to final purchasers), as well as independent sourcing decisions. Both approaches (centralized and decentralized) should lead to the same outcome, and it is likely that firms using each strategy can be found.

Does the BLS export price index capture external or internal prices? The BLS believes it is the external price, that is, the "prices paid by the average foreign buyer."[21] Research testing U.S. pricing-to-market behavior routinely assumes this to be the case. We disagree, particularly when it comes to intrafirm exports.

Consider the striking relationship that emerges in figure 2-2, which plots changes between 1985 and 1989 in the ratio of U.S. export to U.S. producer prices for a number of two-digit SIC industries against the share of U.S. multinational exports accounted for by intrafirm trade.[22] The higher the share accounted for by intrafirm trade, the more closely export price changes match domestic price changes. If the BLS were really capturing prices to final purchasers in foreign countries, one would not expect to find this relationship. Indeed, intrafirm trade is concentrated in the more oligopolistic sectors more likely to be dominated by pricing-to-market practices. Furthermore, where a higher share of U.S. multinational exports is sold at arm's length, export prices do tend to reflect local market conditions: measured in U.S. dollars, prices in the period under consideration rose in response to the exchange rate. By contrast, there is almost no change in the relative export prices of goods sold

**Figure 2-2.** *Change in Real U.S. Export Prices and Share of Intrafirm Trade for Manufacturing Industries, 1985–89*[a]

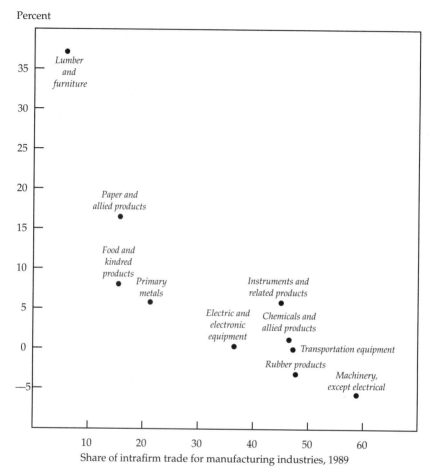

Percent

Source: Intrafirm share data are from *USDIA: 1989 Benchmark Survey, Preliminary Results* (1991), table 85, cols. 6 and 14; and *USDIA: 1988* (1991), table 57, cols. 1 and 4. Producer prices are from U.S. Department of Labor, Bureau of Labor Statistics, *Monthly Labor Review*, vol. 114 (January 1991), table 36, p.108. Export prices are from Bureau of Labor Statistics, "U.S. Export Price Indexes for Selected Categories of Goods," unpublished printout made available by the department's International Price Program (goods categorized by SITC).

a. U.S. export prices are deflated using sectoral producer price indexes.

in industries with larger shares of intrafirm trade; their prices apparently moved in line with U.S. producer prices.

There are four good reasons to think that U.S. export prices and U.S. domestic prices move together in industries with a high share of multinational trade:

—*Efficiency.* Particularly if pricing decisions are decentralized, the export price that the U.S. firm is likely to use will be a cost-plus version that serves as a marginal cost proxy for its allocation decisions.[23]

—*Tax regulation.* When transfer pricing practices are monitored by tax authorities, the price at which arm's-length sales are made in the United States is the measure most acceptable to those authorities in most source and destination nations.

—*Administrative convenience.* Because the pricing report to the BLS comes from the U.S. parent, it will be easier to report the domestic wholesale price than the price actually paid by the foreign buyer, particularly if the foreign subsidiary has some pricing authority. Moreover, BLS policy dictates that "if it is determined . . . that the buyer and seller are affiliated and that the transaction price . . . does not mirror market trends," then the price data will not be collected.[24] But the "market trends" that are readily available to the person filling out the BLS report in the United States are more likely to be the U.S. wholesale or list prices than the prices paid by the unaffiliated foreign buyer to the affiliated seller in a foreign country.[25]

—*Tariffs.* In the face of a currency depreciation, firms have an incentive to save on ad valorem taxes and use the foreign equivalent of the U.S. price, rather than the higher foreign transaction price. (Of course, in the case of an appreciation they would prefer the foreign price.)[26]

The first two of these explanations, efficiency and tax regulation, apply particularly to the intrafirm trade of multinationals, while the other two, administrative convenience and duties, apply to all exports. The evidence in figure 2-2 suggests the first two explanations are the more important: changes in the price measures reported to the BLS by firms with a substantial share of intrafirm trade are more likely to reflect changes in the marginal cost of sourcing in the United States than the prices paid by the average foreign buyer. Once firms are reporting such prices as representative of their intrafirm trade, they are unlikely to report a different price for their trade in the same products that are sold to other locations at arm's length.

If these assumptions are correct, are the export price data "wrong"? Not necessarily. In fact, *both* the internal and external prices are relevant to the firms' adjustment process. Given constant marginal costs, the *external* price is relevant for adjustments along the demand curves of final purchasers; the *internal* price is relevant for adjustments along the derived demand curve for exported inputs used in affiliate sourcing. The full adjustment to an exchange rate change by a multinational company will therefore reflect both types of movements. Moreover, if firms do report changes in their domestic wholesale price, they are likely to be giving a fairly accurate picture of changes in their marginal costs. As a first approximation, if the product contains no imported inputs and marginal cost is constant, its dollar marginal cost will not change in response to the exchange rate. If, however, marginal costs do change—either because of changes in input prices or changes in quantities produced where supply is not infinitely elastic—those changes will resemble changes in the domestic price. Indeed, if the domestic price is a constant markup over marginal costs, changes in domestic prices will give an accurate picture of changes in marginal cost, even though levels will differ. Accordingly, changes in the domestic wholesale price will generally be a useful proxy for changes in the marginal cost relevant for intrafirm sourcing decisions.

## U.S. Trade and Multinational Activity

In the United States, the exporting of manufactured products is heavily concentrated in a relatively small number of large, multinational firms. In 1990 America's top fifty exporters, all multinationals, accounted for nearly 40 percent of U.S. manufacturing exports.[27] For the same year, manufacturing firms with sales exceeding $500 million (that is, large firms), though making up only 20 percent of all exporters in the *Compustat* database (which contains more than 1,000 exporting firms), accounted for 93.2 percent of the total exports of all reporting firms.[28] According to the U.S. Department of Commerce, U.S. parents of multinational enterprises accounted for nearly 80 percent of U.S. manufacturing exports in 1989.[29]

### Multinationals

Also in 1989, intrafirm trade accounted for 39 percent of U.S. manufactured exports.[30] As figure 2-3 shows, if aircraft exports (almost all of which are made at arm's length) are excluded, the intrafirm share in U.S. manufactured exports jumps to 43.3 percent. About three-fourths of these intrafirm exports were sent by U.S. parents to their majority-owned foreign affiliates, with the balance going between U.S. affiliates and their foreign parents. In general, U.S. multinationals ship about half of all their exports intrafirm to their own affiliates abroad.[31] As the last bar in figure 2-3 shows, 82 percent of the intrafirm exports sent by U.S. parents to their foreign manufacturing affiliates were inputs awaiting further value added (as opposed to finished products for resale without further manufacture).

Although multinationals loom large in U.S. exports, exports do not loom large in the overall foreign sales of U.S. multinationals. In 1989 arm's-length exports accounted for only 22 percent of the

**Figure 2-3.** *Intrafirm Manufacturing Exports of U.S. Multinationals, 1989*[a]

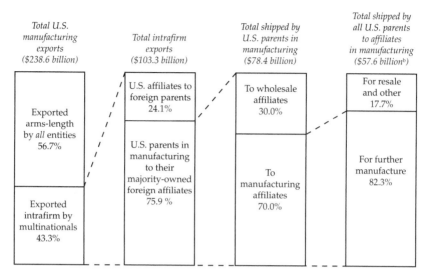

Source: U.S. manufacturing export data are from U.S. Department of Commerce, Bureau of Census, and U.S. Department of Labor, Bureau of Labor Statistics, *Trade & Employment: 3rd Quarter* (1992), table 5. Intrafirm data are from U.S. Department of Commerce, Bureau of Economic Analysis, *U.S. Direct Investment Abroad: 1989, Preliminary Results* (1991), table 85, col. 6; table 71, cols. 6–9; and U.S. Department of Commerce, Bureau of Economic Analysis, *Foreign Direct Investment in the U.S.: 1989* (1991), table G-1, cols. 1, 2, and 4.

a. Excludes aircraft.

b. This number includes exports shipped by nonmanufacturing parents to manufacturing affiliates and is hence larger than implied in the box to the immediate left.

total sales that U.S. multinationals in manufacturing made to unaffiliated foreign customers.[32] In other words, the central channel through which U.S. firms reach their foreign customers and compete internationally is not exports, but foreign-affiliate production and sales. Furthermore, products that are made and sold by the foreign manufacturing affiliates of U.S. parents have a low level of inputs sourced in the United States (see chapter 3).

These data support two of our key points. First, U.S. export behavior cannot be adequately explained without taking into account the role of multinationals in general and intrafirm exports in particular. Second, in analyzing the behavior of "U.S. firms," a distinction needs to be made between U.S.-based firms and U.S.-owned firms. A significant share of U.S. exports is ultimately priced and sold not by firms located in the United States, but by their foreign affiliates. U.S. *export* prices, therefore, may not be the most appropriate data for answering the strategy-laden question of whether the goods sold abroad by American-owned firms to final purchasers are priced to market. This question can only be answered by moving beyond U.S. *export* prices to the second-stage *external* prices that arm's-length foreign customers are charged by the foreign affiliates of U.S. firms. Changes in the exchange rate and other U.S.-based costs provide an opportunity to explore this external pricing.

## Do U.S. Multinationals Price to Market?

American multinationals are concentrated in oligopolistic, high-technology industries (including chemicals, machinery, and scientific instruments). In these industries, American firms have considerable market power arising both from their technological superiority and from their large size. According to standard price theory, monopolist firms in such circumstances will set their prices so that the markup they charge over marginal cost is inversely related to the price elasticity of the demand they face.[33] If this elasticity is constant, the markup will remain constant, and prices and marginal costs will change proportionately.

For ease of exposition, consider the case of a U.S. multinational that is a monopolist in its market abroad. Assume it faces an inverse demand function, $P = f(Q)$, and a cost function, $C(Q)e + C^*(Q)$, where $P$ is the price in foreign currency terms, $Q$ is the quantity sold abroad, $C$ is the cost incurred in the United States (in dollars), $e$ is the nominal exchange rate defined as foreign currency units per U.S. dollar, and $C^*$ is the cost (in foreign currency terms) incurred in the foreign country (where the market is located). The firm will set prices so as to maximize its profits, which can be written in foreign currency units as

(2-1) $$\pi = PQ - Ce - C^*.$$

The standard first-order condition for this firm can be written as

(2-2) $$P = \frac{\eta}{\eta + 1} [C'e + C^*'],$$

where $\eta$ is the price elasticity, and the cost terms represent the marginal cost incurred in the United States and abroad in foreign currency terms. Assuming that the monopolists' marginal cost is constant, we can get

(2-3) $$\Delta P = \Delta\lambda(C'e + C^*') + \lambda C'\Delta e,$$

where $\lambda$ is the monopolist's markup over marginal costs and is equal to $\eta/(\eta + 1)$.

From (2-2), we can also express the firm's price-cost margin, $PCM = (P - (C'e + C^*'))/P$, as follows:

(2-4) $$PCM = \frac{1}{-\eta}.$$

Standard oligopoly theory will lead to an analogous result in which industry concentration and conjectural variations about the responses of other firms will also enter on the right-hand side.[34] Equation (2-4), in turn, will allow us to express the percentage change in $PCM$ as

(2-5) $$\%\Delta PCM = \frac{\partial \eta}{-\eta}.$$

Equation (2-5) says that changes in the monopolist's price-cost margin are a function of changes in the elasticity of demand. If the demand elasticity is constant (that is, $\partial\eta = 0$), then regardless of changes in exchange rates or marginal costs, the monopolist will not change its price-cost margin (at least in the static case). By definition then, such a firm will fully pass through changes in these variables to its foreign prices.

In other words, if $\eta$ is constant, then $\Delta P/\Delta e$, the pass-through rate with respect to the exchange rate will be a constant equal to $\lambda C'$, and the pass-through elasticity with respect to the exchange rate change will be just equal to the U.S. share in the total value added (that is, equal to $\theta$ where $\theta = \lambda C'e/P$). If all value were added in the United States, or if this elasticity were measured on a value-added share-weighted basis, then the pass-through elasticity would be 1, signifying full pass-through.

In "normal" cases (for example, a linear demand curve), however, demand becomes more elastic as price rises. When costs fall, the changes will be reflected in lower prices; but, since demand becomes less elastic, firms raise their markups, and thus prices fall proportionally less than costs.[35] The converse applies for rising prices and costs. In general, oligopolistic exporters would experience rising profit margins when the exchange rate depreciates and falling profit margins when the exchange rate appreciates. When such behavior is destination-specific (that is, when it leads to a divergence between changes in prices at home and abroad), then the firm is "pricing to market," and, as noted above, such behavior appears to be a feature of foreign exporters.[36]

These considerations normally lead to a testing framework using a cost-plus-markup specification.[37] If one were to follow the tradition of the existing literature in studying the foreign price behavior of U.S. multinationals, the next step would be to regress the final product prices of these enterprises on their U.S. and foreign costs, as in equation (2-3). However, explicit price data for the foreign sales of U.S. multinationals are not available, although these prices could be estimated using some assumptions about how U.S. multi-nationals' volume of sales abroad moved and then applying the standard formulation.[38] An alternative approach would be to test the model using the price-cost margin specification, which is the approach taken here.

We specify and estimate a function in which we regress changes in the price-cost margin against changes in U.S. and foreign costs, and foreign competitor prices. We assume

$$(2\text{-}6) \qquad \Delta PCM = f(\Delta \tilde{e}, \Delta C', \Delta C^{*\prime}, \Delta F^*),$$

where $C'$ is the portion of the marginal cost incurred in the United States, $\tilde{e}$ is the nominal exchange rate in dollars per unit of foreign currency (that is, equal to $1/e$), $C^{*\prime}$ is the portion of the marginal cost incurred in the foreign country, and $F^*$ is the price charged by foreign competitors. We then specify a linearized version:

$$(2\text{-}7) \quad \%\Delta PCM_{it} = \psi_0 + \psi_1 \%\Delta \tilde{e}_{it} + \psi_2 \%\Delta PPI_{it}^{US} + \psi_3 \%\Delta PPI_{it}^* + \omega,$$

where $i$ is an industry subscript and $t$ is a period subscript, and *PPI* refers to the producer price index. We assume that $\Delta PPI_i^{US}$ reflects changes in industry-specific U.S.-based marginal costs, and that $\Delta PPI_i^*$ reflects changes both in foreign-based marginal costs and in foreign competitors' prices. Exchange rates are nominal, weight-averaged, industry-specific rates measured in dollars per unit of foreign currency. Foreign producer prices are weight-averaged, industry-specific producer prices (from country sources). Weights for both variables are based on the country shares in total sales of each industry in the nine major countries that U.S. majority-owned foreign affiliates (MOFAs) operate in.[39]

We can see from equation (2-5) that the dependent variable, $\%\Delta PCM$, will be equal to the percentage change in the elasticity of demand. Thus if the demand elasticity (and the markup) were constant, then none of the coefficients in equation (2-7) would be different from zero. This is what would be expected under the conventional wisdom that U.S. firms simply pass-through exchange rate and other costs into their foreign prices.

If in fact American firms do price to market—that is, if they raise their price-cost margins when the dollar depreciates—then one would expect to find a statistically significant positive coefficient on the exchange rate (since ẽ is measured in dollars per unit of foreign currency). Similarly, with such pricing-to-market behavior, higher U.S. costs would be associated with a reduction in price-cost margins and a negative coefficient on this variable is expected. By the same logic, higher foreign costs would raise the price-cost margins, leading to a positive coefficient.[40]

### Estimation

The basic equation was estimated for data on U.S. majority-owned foreign affiliates in fourteen manufacturing industries. Each observation is a year-to-year percentage change in the dependent and independent variables for each industry. The model is first estimated for the period 1982–89.[41] Price-cost margins for individual industries are calculated under the assumption that marginal cost is equal to average variable cost for each firm.[42] Thus

$$(2\text{-}8) \qquad PCM_i = \frac{Sales_i - COGS_i}{Sales_i},$$

where COGS stands for costs of goods sold and includes labor and material costs. Dividing each term on the right-hand side of (2-8) by the quantity sold gives

$$(2\text{-}9) \qquad PCM_i = \frac{P_i - AVC_i}{P_i},$$

which is the ratio of industry gross profit to revenue.

**Table 2-1.** *Price-Cost Margins of U.S. Majority-Owned Foreign Affiliates in Selected Industries, 1985*

Ratio

| Industry | Price-cost margin |
|---|---|
| Manufacturing | 0.22 |
| Food and kindred products | 0.27 |
| Beverages | 0.42 |
| Chemicals and allied products | 0.28 |
| Industrial chemicals and synthetics | 0.15 |
| Drugs | 0.44 |
| Primary and fabricated metals | 0.20 |
| Machinery except electrical | 0.31 |
| Office and computing machines | 0.37 |
| Electric and electronic equipment | 0.19 |
| Household appliances | 0.28 |
| Electronic components and accessories | 0.15 |
| Motor vehicles and equipment | 0.08 |
| Tobacco products | 0.36 |
| Lumber and furniture | 0.19 |
| Printing and publishing | 0.45 |
| Glass products | 0.19 |
| Instruments and related products | 0.27 |

Source: Authors' estimates based on data from *USDIA: 1985* (1988), table 28.

To give a flavor of the variation by industry in the dependent variable, the estimated 1985 price-cost margins of U.S. MOFAs for a variety of industries are shown in table 2-1. The price-cost margins estimated for U.S. MOFAs appear reasonable, as gauged by the demand elasticities and Herfindahl indexes they imply (under assumptions of Cournot competition).[43]

For instance, while the monopoly outcome is ruled out for almost all industries, the very high price-cost margins in beverages and drugs reflects very high concentration ratios (and perhaps low price elasticity in the case of drugs). By contrast, the very low margins for U.S. MOFAs in the automobile industry are affected in part by the fact that they were lower than usual in 1985 (the margins had risen to more than 12 percent by 1989) and partly reflect the high price elasticities faced by producers in this industry.[44]

### Results

Estimates of equation (2-7) are reported in table 2-2 for the dollar depreciation, appreciation, and overall period between 1982 and 1989. In general the estimated coefficients on the exchange rate variable provide strong support for the pricing-to-market hypothesis and rejection of the full pass-through view. The estimated magnitudes (which range from 0.31 to 0.60) appear plausible, and with one exception (specification 4), the coefficients differ from zero by an amount judged statistically significant in the standard sense. Furthermore, as one might anticipate, the results imply that pass-through behavior in response to changes in the exchange rate is quite similar to that in response to changes in U.S. costs (see specifications 2 and 5, in particular).[45]

The results in specification 4, the 1982–85 appreciation phase, appear weakest. But when tested for coefficient stability, specifications 1, 3, and 4 easily pass the standard Chow test.[46] Thus, although the results in specification 4 taken alone do not allow us to reject the hypothesis that American firms practiced full pass-through during the 1982–85 period, the results of the Chow test do not allow us to reject the hypothesis that American firms responded similarly to the dollar appreciation and depreciation. Besides, convincing evidence is available to show that, over the period as a whole, the hypothesis of complete pass-through can be rejected. Last, but not least, the pass-through behavior implied by these results (discussed in a moment) are well within the range of those reported in the literature for foreign (exporting) firms competing in U.S. markets.[47] It appears that U.S. firms are not so different after all.

**Table 2-2.** *Regressions Explaining Changes in Price-Cost Margins of U.S. Majority-Owned Foreign Affiliates in Manufacturing, 1983–89*[a]

| Independent variable[b] | Dollar depreciating, 1986–89 | Dollar depreciating, 1986–89 | Entire period, 1983–89 | Dollar appreciating, 1983–85 | Entire period, 1983–89 |
|---|---|---|---|---|---|
| Constant | -0.40 (-0.16) | 0.60 (0.28) | 0.57 (0.36) | 1.54 (0.35) | -3.28 (-1.17) |
| Nominal exchange rate[c] | 0.44 (3.17) | ... | 0.31 (3.42) | 0.60 (0.94) | 0.54 (3.54) |
| U.S. producer prices[d] | -0.16 (-0.52) | ... | -0.44 (-1.78) | -0.51 (-0.99) | -0.49 (-2.67) |
| Exchange rate/U.S. producer prices | ... | 0.38 (3.47) | ... | ... | ... |
| Foreign producer prices[d] | 0.17 (0.31) | 0.26 (0.51) | 0.73 (1.83) | 1.17 (1.76) | 1.64 (1.93) |
| *Summary statistics* | | | | | |
| Adjusted $R^2$ | 0.17 | 0.18 | 0.10 | 0.01 | 0.89 |
| Number of observations | 56 | 56 | 98 | 42 | 7 |

Source: Authors' regressions using nominal exchange rate data from International Monetary Fund, *International Financial Statistics Yearbook* (rf quotes). Data on country shares by industry are from *USDIA: 1989 Benchmark Survey, Preliminary Results* (1991), table 33. U.S. and foreign industry-specific producer price change data are estimated from Organization of Economic Cooperation and Development, *Indicators of Industrial Activity*, various issues.

a. The regressions are based on equation (2-7) in the text. The dependent variable is the percentage change in the price-cost margin. The numbers in parentheses are *t*-statistics. Manufacturing industries included in the regression are food and kindred products; chemicals and allied products; fabricated metal products; machinery except electrical; electric and electronic products; motor vehicles and equipment; tobacco products; textile products and apparel; lumber and furniture; paper and allied products; printing and publishing; glass products; stone, clay, and related; and instruments and related.

b. All independent variables are expressed as year-to-year percent changes.

c. The nominal exchange rate is defined as dollars per unit of foreign currency. Industry-specific exchange rates are fixed-weight average changes in nominal exchange rates across the nine major countries (see text) that host U.S. majority-owned foreign affiliates (MOFAs). Country weights for each industry are based on 1989 country shares in U.S. MOFAs' sales in that particular country.

d. Producer prices are for the fixed-weight index of manufactured goods, excluding computers. Country weights used for estimating changes in industry-specific foreign producer prices are the same as those used above for estimating exchange rate changes.

In order to help interpret the results shown in table 2-2, we provide a simulation spreadsheet in table 2-3, which takes the coefficients on the exchange rate and uses them to impute exchange rate pass-through ratios. The 1985 data on the cost structure of U.S. MOFAs provide the initial conditions. As shown, U.S. costs accounted for 15.5 percent of value added and 20 percent of total cost of goods sold. From equation (2-4), if U.S. MOFAs were all monopolies in their respective foreign markets, then their average price-cost margin of 0.224 corresponds to a demand elasticity of 4.46. In the more realistic case of oligopoly, with a Herfindahl index of 0.25, these data correspond to a demand elasticity of 1.12 (see the last line of table 2-3).

Table 2-3 shows what effect a 10 percent decline in the U.S. dollar's exchange rate would have on foreign currency prices under the different elasticities of the price-cost margin estimated in table 2-2. Consider the first column in table 2-3 when the elasticity of the price-cost margin with respect to U.S. costs is taken to be zero (which represents the extreme form of the conventional wisdom). In this case, we know that the *PCM* will remain unchanged. Hence, given a 20 percent share in total costs of goods sold, the 10 percent fall in the dollar lowers the total costs of goods sold by 2 percent. With the markup unchanged, prices also fall by 2 percent, giving a pass-through rate equal to unity. Note, however, that because of the small U.S. share in total value added, even under complete pass-through, the foreign currency prices charged by U.S. multinationals decline by just 2 percent in the face of a 10 percent fall in the U.S. dollar.

We then go on to simulate cases in which the *PCM* elasticity corresponds to the exchange rate change coefficients (from smallest to largest) that we have estimated in our regressions in table 2-2. With a *PCM* elasticity of 0.31 (taken from specification 3 in table 2-2), prices decline by only 1.13 rather than 2.00 percent, as under full pass-through. This implies a pass-through rate of 0.56. With a *PCM*

Table 2-3. *Simulating the Pass-Through Response of U.S. Majority-Owned Foreign Affiliates to a 10 Percent Decline in the U.S. dollar*[a]

| Item | Price-cost margin elasticity[b] | | | | | |
|---|---|---|---|---|---|---|
| | 0.00 | 0.31 | 0.38 | 0.44 | 0.54 | 0.60 |
| New price-cost margin[c] | 0.22 | 0.23 | 0.23 | 0.23 | 0.24 | 0.24 |
| New price[d] | 0.98 | 0.99 | 0.99 | 0.99 | 1.00 | 1.00 |
| Percent change in costs | −2.00 | −2.00 | −2.00 | −2.00 | −2.00 | −2.00 |
| Percent change in price | −2.00 | −1.13 | −0.91 | −0.74 | −0.45 | −0.27 |
| Pass-through rate[e] | 1.00 | 0.56 | 0.46 | 0.37 | 0.22 | 0.14 |
| Imputed demand elasticity[f] | 1.12 | 1.08 | 1.08 | 1.07 | 1.06 | 1.05 |

Source: Authors' calculations based on results from table 2-2 and *USDIA: 1985* (1988), table 28, col. 1 and 7, and table 51, col. 1.

a. Initial U.S. and foreign costs in 1985 accounted for 15.5 and 62.1 percent, respectively, of total value added. The difference of 22.4 percent represented the initial price-cost margin.

b. These price-cost margin elasticities are based on regressions shown in table 2-2.

c. The new price-cost margin (PCM) equals (initial PCM) * [1.0 + (0.10 * PCM elasticity)].

d. The new price equals (new costs) / (1.0 − new PCM), where new costs equal (initial U.S. costs * 0.90) plus initial foreign costs.

e. The pass-through rate is the percentage change in price divided by the percentage change in costs.

f. The imputed demand elasticity is an assumed Herfindahl index value of 0.25 divided by the new price-cost margin.

elasticity of 0.38 (taken from specification 2 in table 2-2), prices decline by only 0.91, which implies a pass-through rate of 0.46. In general, larger *PCM* elasticities result in smaller pass-through and larger changes in markups.

The actual real depreciation of the U.S. dollar between 1985 and 1989 was 35 percent. Given the 20 percent share of U.S. costs (in the total), even if U.S. firms had fully passed through this exchange rate change into their final sales prices, on average their prices in foreign markets would have declined by just 7 percent. In fact, given the estimated *PCM* elasticity of 0.31 in specification 3 (in table 2-2), the average decline in prices would have been just (0.56 * 7 percent), that is, just 3.9 percent. It is perhaps no wonder that even in the face of this major exchange rate shift, a majority of the U.S. exporting firms surveyed indicated they had "maintained" their foreign currency prices.

Of course, if U.S. products were simply distributed by U.S. foreign affiliates, the price declines, although a small share of total sales, would be more conspicuous than if they were intermediate inputs and thus a small share of the value of each final product sold. But, in fact, the 1989 data indicate that 82 percent of the imports received by U.S. MOFAs in the manufacturing industry are inputs for further value added, which supports the interpretation that these products are intermediate inputs rather than final sales.

## Further Tests

Following the analysis just described, we went back to the 1966 (benchmark) survey on the foreign operations of U.S. multinationals conducted by the U.S. Department of Commerce's Bureau of Economic Analysis and estimated price-cost margins for the foreign operations of U.S. multinationals. We also made these estimates for the years 1990–94. A subset of the estimates appears in table 2-4. In making comparisons over time, one must keep in mind that the estimates are not for a fixed sample of firms. The pattern is then rather clear: price-cost margins declined sharply between 1966 and 1977. This decline is most visible in transportation equipment (where margins apparently continued to fall between 1977 and 1982). The estimates in office and computing equipment as well indicate a marked and steady decline between 1977 and 1994. Such a decline is also visible in the electronics sector. At the same time, U.S. multinationals continue to maintain high price-cost margins in beverages, drugs, and printing and publishing. The post-1966 declines in price-cost margins are not inconsistent with the catch-up and competition that U.S. firms have faced from competitors in other developed countries and (especially in machinery and electronics) from new entrants at home.

**Table 2-4.** *Price-Cost Margins of U.S. Majority-Owned Foreign Affiliates in Selected Industries, 1966–94*

Percent

| Industry | Price-cost margin | | | | | |
|---|---|---|---|---|---|---|
| | 1966 | 1977 | 1982 | 1985 | 1989 | 1994 |
| Manufacturing | 39 | 24 | 22 | 22 | 26 | 24 |
| Food and kindred products | 30 | 26 | 27 | 27 | 32 | 32 |
| Grain mill and bakery products | | 21 | 24 | 23 | 32 | 31 |
| Beverages | | 46 | 40 | 42 | 44 | 44 |
| Chemicals and allied products | 40 | 30 | 28 | 28 | 35 | 33 |
| Industrial chemicals and synthetics | | 16 | 15 | 15 | 25 | 22 |
| Drugs | | 43 | 44 | 44 | 48 | 47 |
| Soaps, cleaners, and toilet goods | | 40 | 42 | 40 | 42 | 43 |
| Agricultural chemicals | | 19 | 26 | 24 | 26 | 29 |
| Primary and fabricated metals | 40 | 19 | 18 | 20 | 23 | 20 |
| Primary metal industries | | 19 | 10 | 14 | 18 | 14 |
| Ferrous | | 17 | 18 | 18 | 9 | 14 |
| Nonferrous | | 19 | 6 | 12 | 21 | 14 |
| Fabricated metal products | | 19 | 21 | 22 | 25 | 22 |
| Machinery except electrical | 45 | 35 | 30 | 31 | 30 | 25 |
| Farm and garden machinery | | 14 | 4 | 15 | 11 | 8 |
| Construction and related | | 19 | 23 | 18 | 18 | 18 |
| Office and computing machines | | 47 | 39 | 37 | | 27 |
| Electric and electronic equipment | | 25 | 22 | 19 | 19 | 17 |
| Household appliances | | 30 | 25 | 28 | 21 | 20 |
| Radio, TV, and communication | | 18 | 18 | 20 | 26 | 20 |
| Electronic components and accessories | | 18 | 18 | 15 | 16 | 14 |
| Transportation equipment | 32 | 13 | 7 | 9 | 12 | 11 |
| Motor vehicles and equipment | | 11 | 6 | 8 | 12 | 10 |
| Other | | 24 | 27 | 24 | 13 | 20 |
| Other manufacturing | 43 | 26 | 26 | 27 | 29 | 27 |
| Tobacco products | | 27 | 33 | 36 | 36 | 38 |
| Textile products and apparel | | 27 | 21 | 22 | 27 | 22 |
| Lumber and furniture | | 17 | 18 | 19 | 21 | 21 |
| Paper and allied products | | 27 | 26 | 29 | 30 | 23 |
| Printing and publishing | | 45 | 45 | 45 | 44 | 42 |
| Rubber products | | 18 | 20 | 19 | 19 | 21 |
| Miscellaneous plastics | | 40 | 25 | 28 | 27 | 27 |
| Glass products | | 21 | 18 | 19 | 28 | 23 |
| Stone, clay, and related products | | 21 | 24 | 24 | 28 | 24 |
| Instruments and related products | | 30 | 28 | 27 | 31 | 30 |

Source: Authors' estimates based on data from *USDIA*, various issues.

Using these extended data, we estimated equation (2-7) for the period 1983–94 (the years for which continuous annual data are available). In that regression, the nominal exchange rate takes a coefficient of 0.20 ($t$-stat, 2.61), which (on the basis of the imputation described in table 2-3) implies a pass-through rate of 0.72. Altogether, then, the estimated results suggest pass-through rates of 15 to 70 percent. The size of these estimates is consistent with those made by other researchers for foreign firms competing in U.S. markets.[48]

To summarize, the results presented in this chapter strongly suggest that U.S. firms vary their price-cost margins abroad in response to changes in the dollar's exchange rate. This finding is consistent not only with theory (see appendix A) but also with firm-level case studies that we have conducted (see appendix B). And it refutes the view that U.S. firms fail to price to market.

# Sourcing Responses of U.S. Multinationals | 3

THIS CHAPTER TAKES up the question of whether U.S. multinationals and foreign multinationals operating in the United States might be shifting production across borders in response to changes in real exchange rates. Do they actually exhibit such operational flexibility, and what light does their behavior shed on the hysteresis hypothesis regarding U.S. manufacturing? According to that hypothesis, the high dollar of the first half of the 1980s caused U.S. competitiveness to erode in such a fashion that the drop in the dollar during the second half of 1980s was not sufficient to bring back the manufacturing value added that had by then left the United States. The validity of this hypothesis can be tested by examining whether U.S. and foreign firms increased their relative reliance on U.S. capacity after the drop in the dollar.

This chapter draws on Subramanian Rangan, "Do Multinationals Operate Flexibly? Theory and Evidence," *Journal of International Business Studies,* vol. 29, no. 2 (1998), pp. 217–37. We thank the *Journal of International Business Studies* for permission.

The production-shifting behavior of foreign multinationals in the United States also provides an opportunity to explore the "Japan is different" hypothesis, which posits that despite the "endaka" (or sharp appreciation of the yen in relation to the U.S. dollar), Japanese multinationals operating in the United States are still relying heavily on Japanese content. Some observers see this as mercantilist behavior, whereas others call it a "vintage" effect of the relative newness of Japanese multinational operations on the U.S. scene. With the passage of time and the aging of those operations, they argue, U.S. content will rise. The relevant patterns of behavior over time and the competing explanations for them are sorted out in this chapter. Attention is also given to the sourcing responses of U.S. multinationals in some developing economies.

The main purpose in following these various lines of discussion is to explore two larger questions: To what extent are geographic locations close substitutes? And, viewed from a micro (or firm) perspective, are exchange rates an effective policy instrument for achieving international macroeconomic adjustment? According to the McKinnon-Mundell school of thought, geographic locations are close substitutes and exchange rates ought not to be deployed in efforts to achieve macro adjustment. However, this view is not borne out by the evidence reviewed in this chapter. Although changes in exchange rates do work, it is more optimal to let the adjustment process be driven by changes in nominal exchange rates rather than by changes in prices (which would have to be large, and hence could be more destabilizing and less feasible, especially on the downward side).

## Do Multinationals Operate "Flexibly"?

Exchange rate changes do not figure high on the list of reasons for multinational enterprises (MNEs) to locate operations abroad. But, as a long list of scholars have noted, once MNEs do locate their operations in two or more currency areas, they may, in many respects, be well-positioned to exploit changes in exchange rates.[1] In addition to hedging in currency markets, flexing profit margins, and improving productivity, MNEs may respond to real exchange rate changes by shifting sourcing and production within their networks to areas made more competitive by these changes.

This is the thrust of operational flexibility, a belief that MNEs have "greater degrees of freedom than a uni-national firm confined to one country."[2] Indeed, some multinational management scholars have argued that the essence or "the incremental value" of being multinational lies in operational flexibility.[3]

Some of these same scholars, however, have expressed misgivings about management's actual ability to perceive the flexibility options latent in international networks.[4] They also wonder whether MNEs possess the organizational wherewithal to pursue those options, arguing that "having the potential to exercise flexibility is a far cry from having the management system to do it."[5] Organizational inertia and high coordination costs are cited as further impediments to operational flexibility.

In the abstract, arguments can be made on both sides of the flexibility question, but empirical work is required to explore the issue directly.[6] The question of whether U.S., European, and Japanese MNEs operate flexibly is best explored in the "natural experiment" setting provided by the massive swings in the U.S. dollar since the late 1970s (see figures 3-1 and 3-2). Three hypotheses about flexibility—which might be labeled flexibility optimism, flexibility pessimism, and flexibility realism—can be drawn from the theoretical literature for empirical analysis.

### Flexibility Optimism

Flexibility optimism rests on the premise that MNE facilities in countries with different exchange rates are adequately integrated

**Figure 3-1.** *Trade-Weighted Exchange Rate of the U.S. Dollar, 1977–94*

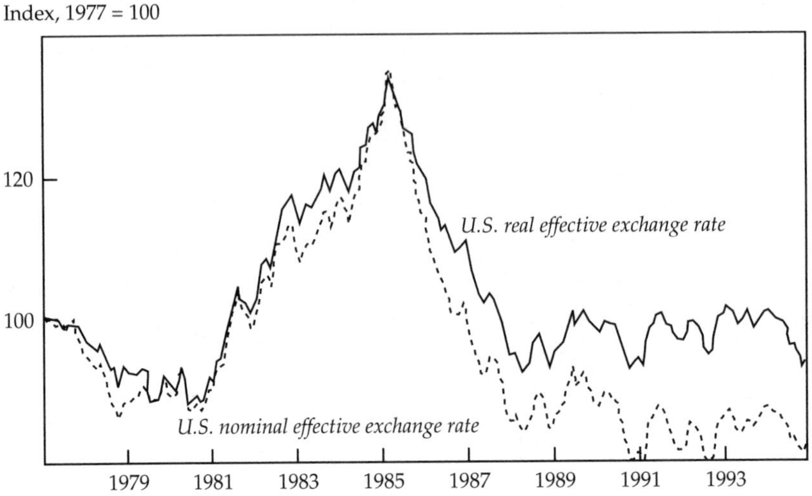

Index, 1977 = 100

Source: J. P. Morgan.

in terms of intrafirm product and information flows.[7] Once an MNE has incurred sunk costs to establish plants in another currency area, the home facility in principle has access to output produced abroad at something close to foreign marginal costs. Routine operation of the foreign facility also generates a set of business relationships, a continually replenished stock of information about actual prices, and information about the existence, location, and precise needs and capabilities of buyers and suppliers in that region. The MNE thereby enjoys certain sunk-cost advantages and privileged access to information and connections in multiple currency areas.[8]

Another assumption of flexibility optimism is that under current production technologies in manufacturing industries, a sizable proportion of production costs are not fixed (but are variable) and hence possibly "movable." Material inputs are estimated to account for 25 percent of total costs for the typical manufacturing firm.[9] And since changes in exchange rates take long periods of time to be fully

**Figure 3-2.** *U.S. Dollar in Relation to the Japanese Yen and the German Mark, 1977–94*

Index, 1977 = 100

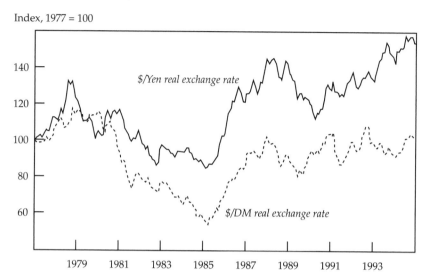

Source: IMF, *International Financial Statistics,* CD-ROM (March 1996).

reflected in national prices (that is, until exchange rates revert to initial levels in "real" terms), there is, ceteris paribus, an opportunity for MNEs to create cost savings by shifting sourcing and production at the margin to existing plants in locations favored by the exchange rate change. Of course, MNEs' expectations about the future will shape their operating decisions. But when it comes to forecasting exchange rate movements, even specialists have been unable to do better than a random-walk model.[10] That is why operational flexibility is said to engender a valuable "option."[11]

At the same time, switching costs, the possible loss of plant scale economies, higher inventory and working capital costs, transport and tariff costs, and the availability (in particular, the lack) of suitable capacity are all taken into account under this hypothesis. But these factors simply imply that exchange rates will have to cross a certain threshold (that is, the changes may have to be sizable) before switching becomes optimal. Accordingly, the flexibility-optimism hypothesis may be expressed as follows: *units within multinational enterprises in manufacturing industries will exhibit sizable sourcing and production shifting behavior, especially in response to large changes in real exchange rates.*

Flexibility optimism derives in good measure from the view that the MNE is a unified rational entity whose subunits operate to optimize firm-wide performance. This position is no doubt consistent with the idea that MNEs are global hierarchies that internalize foreign operations with the intention of controlling them.[12]

### Flexibility Pessimism

Another important reality is that the full-fledged foreign affiliates of multinational enterprises, especially those operating in the large markets of the Triad, are also internal organizations in their own right. Foreign affiliates might act to protect their local mandates and resources even if such behavior detracts from the interests of the enterprise as a whole.[13] Employment guarantees are not likely to have much effect either because managers will be concerned about promotion prospects and the loss of status, and thus there may be some reciprocal cross-subsidization among units.[14] In such a case, even units that have become relatively inefficient or expensive (perhaps because of changes in exchange rates) might be allowed to hold on to the full initial complement of resources and responsibilities.

The situation could become worse if internal systems are weak. Although cost accounting and management control systems have been in use since the 1920s, MNEs today are far larger in size and complexity and may not possess the information advantages they need to operate flexibly.[15]

Under the influence of administrative heritage, or a desire to continue doing things in the same old way, firms will tend to maintain the existing allocation of resources, roles, and responsibilities.[16]

Administrative heritage, some say, carries the same weight as economic, political, and other external pressures."[17] It can even lead firms to "maintain for a substantial time production configurations that do not optimize physical production costs."[18]

In sharp contrast to the optimism view, the flexibility-pessimism hypothesis states: *units within multinational enterprises in manufacturing industries will exhibit no noticeable operational responses to changes in real exchange rates; rather, their production and sourcing will appear sticky and unresponsive.*

### Flexibility Realism

Flexibility realism begins with the premise that flexibility is "a property of initial positions."[19] In other words, tappable commonalties and intrafirm linkages (in terms of intermediate inputs, relationships, assets, and labor) must already be in existence. To be flexible in the current period, MNEs need to have planned and invested accordingly in previous periods. Investments in flexibility are seen best not in terms of excess capacity but in terms of opportunity costs. For instance, designing and developing two families of products, one for Europe and the other for North America, might go a long way toward making an MNE locally responsive, but it will reduce the firm's ability to shift production should exchange rates change. In this situation, investing in flexibility might mean forgoing a degree of *local* responsiveness.

At a minimum, a considerable proportion of intermediate inputs will have to be common at both locations. Better still, as a normal practice external suppliers at the two locations should be trained to supply the sister affiliate in the other location. Similarly, operational flexibility will be enhanced if engineers in the two facilities can work on common standards and designs, or if specialized capital assets can tolerate alternate inputs and outputs (and thus become less location-specific). Scenario planning and "flexibility drills" might also be helpful. Without such investments in flexibility, even MNEs seeking to maximize profits will have a hard time staging vigorous responses to changes in exchange rates or other cross-national variables.[20] Up to now, MNEs appear to have given such investments little consideration.

During the 1950s and 1960s MNEs from both Europe and the United States greatly expanded their presence abroad.[21] This was a period of fixed exchange rates, high transport and communication costs, trade protection, and punitive tariffs. MNEs were forced to set up their manufacturing facilities behind tariff walls and to cope with large differences in taste and capability across regions.[22] Because MNE investments in the Triad were primarily of a "market-seeking nature" from the 1950s into the 1970s, local affiliates typically modified products "and even manufacturing processes to meet local needs."[23]

Under the circumstances, management priorities revolved around local markets, local competition, and growth. Multinational managers saw little value in transcontinental operational flexibility, especially because it might have had an adverse effect on local responsiveness. This regional orientation, maintained from the 1950s into the 1970s, did little to stimulate the accumulation of information sets, intermediate and final product portfolios, and physical and human assets that were fully compatible, not to mention fungible, across continents.[24]

In those years, multinational managers had little inkling of the rapid and intense trade liberalization or ensuing global competition that lay just around the corner. Nor could they foresee the enormous advances in transportation and especially telecommunication that would make cross-shipments and international coordination much easier. And who among them would have predicted the sudden arrival of the floating exchange rate regime or the wide swings in exchange rates that would follow? Most of them were certain (and, as it turned out, mistaken) that the fixed exchange rate regime would continue.[25] Even later on, the prevalent view was that floating rates would be much less volatile than they turned out to be.

Hence one would not expect to find a high degree of compatibility across MNEs' dispersed operations. Yet, successful MNEs are known to derive their economic rents from the ownership of firm-specific intangible assets for which they create their own internal markets. Also, one of their key strengths is their effective management of internal markets. They will undoubtedly attempt to fortify that strength when faced with suitable opportunities (such as sizable changes in real exchange rate changes). Accordingly, the flexibility-realism hypothesis states: *units within multinational enterprises in manufacturing industries will exhibit sourcing and production shifting responses, but these responses are likely to be relatively modest even in the face of large changes in real exchange rates.*

To recap, flexibility optimism emphasizes macro efficiency and predicts sizable responses. Flexibility pessimism emphasizes the micro organization and predicts sticky responses. Flexibility realism is sympathetic to economic rationality and efficiency but predicts that MNEs' previous actions and strategies will constrain the vigor with which they can respond. Although the three hypotheses are admittedly crude (and pertain primarily to "horizontal" as opposed to "vertical" multinationals), they comport well with the coarse nature of the available "evidence."

## Exploring Flexibility Empirically

We formulate three conceptual models of multinational sourcing adjustment to exchange rate changes.

*Conceptual Models*

The models are named "complete substitution," "rising switching costs," and "floor and ceiling" (see figure 3-3). They represent

**Figure 3-3.** *Conceptual Models of Multinational Sourcing Responses to Exchange Rate Changes*

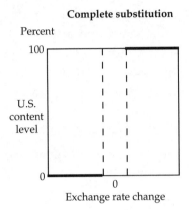

**Complete substitution**

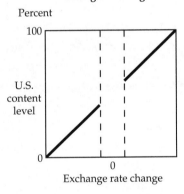

**Rising switching costs**

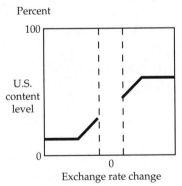

**Floor and ceiling**

the viewpoint of a foreign affiliate of an MNE parent. Suppose it is a German affiliate of an MNE headquartered in the United States and that the X-axis in each panel shows changes in the bilateral real exchange rate between the dollar and the deutsche mark. Real depreciations in the dollar are indicated by shifts to the right of zero, and real appreciations by shifts to the left of zero. To the right of zero, U.S. capacity is becoming relatively more competitive, and to the left it is becoming less competitive. The Y-axis plots the U.S. (or home) content level in products sold in Germany by the German affiliate of the U.S. multinational enterprise.

THE COMPLETE SUBSTITUTION MODEL. The basic assumption of the complete substitution model is that small changes in the exchange rate will not elicit a shift in production because firms have to factor in plant scale economies and switching costs. But if the change is so large that the rate crosses a certain threshold (which is likely to vary by firm, industry, and country), then, even after factoring in switching costs and lost plant scale economies, it will be optimal for firms to shift production, and they will do so completely. Clearly, this model places heavy emphasis on factor costs and predicts that multinationals will adjust in a complete and symmetric manner to changes in real exchange rates that cross the threshold. It might be considered the analytical counterpart of an extreme flexibility-optimism hypothesis.

Thus, when the dollar depreciates in real terms and crosses the switching-cost threshold, foreign production ceases altogether and the foreign market is served from facilities at home. In this extreme case, U.S. content in products sold abroad by U.S.-based MNEs rises to 100 percent. The converse holds when the dollar appreciates beyond the switching threshold. The pattern of adjustment is shown in the top panel in figure 3-3. In reality, of course, the complete substitution model of unbounded adjustment is unlikely to be a good representation of the manner in which MNEs shift production because switching costs are unlikely to be fixed, and (because of reentry costs) complete exit is likely to be rare.

THE RISING SWITCHING COSTS MODEL. This model is far closer to reality than the preceding one. Here, switching costs are likely to be a rising and perhaps convex function of the degree to which switching takes place. In other words, there is likely to be a sequence of switching thresholds, each crossed as the exchange rate moves secularly in a particular direction away from the initial rate. So a 10 percent change in the exchange rate may lead to a small adjustment, a 20 percent change to a larger adjustment, and a 40 percent change to an even larger adjustment (see the middle panel in figure 3-3).

Like the complete substitution model, this model also assumes that adjustment can be unbounded (that is, can go to 100 percent). Of course, it is unlikely that changes in exchange rates alone would cause an MNE to abandon its operations in countries that have become less cost-competitive. The notion that responses are in fact bounded gives rise to the third model.

THE FLOOR AND CEILING MODEL. The floor and ceiling model recognizes thresholds and rising switching costs, but it also postulates that there is a certain level—call it the "floor"—below which home-country content cannot be reduced in the medium run (that is, over the average exchange rate cycle). In the case of a critical or highly scale-intensive input, that level may be determined by historical factors and market size. Or the relative newness of the input may dictate that it be fabricated near the site of innovation and ongoing research, again home. Under such circumstances, changes in the exchange rate may not trigger a shift of the locus of this input's production.

There is also a ceiling above which the home-country content cannot rise in the medium run, say, because certain value-added activities (such as packaging, distribution, sales, and service) have to remain local. Among other factors, the value-to-weight ratio of inputs, tariffs, the degree to which value is added in the provision of services, and local content regulations may all help determine the height of the ceiling.

This model suggests a discontinuous adjustment curve with kinks on either side where the curve slopes from positive to zero. The kinks imply, first, that the responses are bounded (that is, in the time horizon contemplated here, the home-local mix cannot go to 1:0 or 0:1 proportions); second, that given certain initial home-content levels, responses may be asymmetric between appreciations and depreciations. If the initial home-content level is near or at the floor, for instance, even a relatively large appreciation in the home currency is unlikely to elicit switching responses, whereas depreciations that cross the threshold will trigger a rise in home content. Conversely, if the initial home-content level is near or at the ceiling, even large depreciations in the home currency will not elicit much of a response, but threshold-crossing appreciations will.

Of the three models, this third one appears the most plausible, especially if the floors and ceilings are considered endogenous over longer time horizons. To be sure, it will be difficult empirically to distinguish between the rising switching costs model and the floor and ceiling model. To begin with, the shortest time window over which changes can be examined in the data from the U.S. Department of Commerce's Bureau of Economic Analysis (BEA) is one year, which may be a long enough period for firms to shift floors and ceilings. Furthermore, over the sample interval (1977–94) firms may have been operating within the adjustment band (the positive sloped area that is away from either floor or ceiling) and may not have brushed up against either the upper or lower bounds.

### Empirical Evidence, 1977–94

Empirical analysis meets with numerous challenges in exploring firm behavior and its causes. Perhaps the foremost of these is how to operationalize the dependent variable. In other words, what indicator of operational flexibility would be faithful to the purpose and yet be measurable with the available historical data? Naturally, the less the chosen indicator is influenced by factors other than changes in real exchange rates, the better.

One plausible indicator that fits these criteria is *movements in the mix of inputs that go into the products sold by MNEs.* Suppose the German affiliate of a U.S. parent manufactures and sells products in Germany that are made with both local and imported U.S. inputs. Now, imagine that the dollar depreciates substantially in real terms in relation to the deutsche mark. In theory, the effect of the weaker dollar may fail to show up in lower German prices for U.S. imports.[26] But, as empirical studies on export pricing and pass-through have shown (see chapter 2), the bulk of the exchange rate change will be reflected in the local currency price of exports in destination markets.

Accordingly, if our hypothetical MNE is operating flexibly, its German affiliate will alter its input mix, relying more on its U.S. parent to provide intermediate and final products for its German customers. Consequently, the U.S. content in the sales of German affiliates will rise, displacing local German content, which (as a result of the mark's appreciation) will become more expensive. If the firm does not operate flexibly, then shifts in real exchange rates will not be systematically correlated with such substitution behavior in the firm's input mix.

This methodology is attractive for several reasons. First, the measure is a direct variant of the concept of the elasticity of substitution. This latter concept is the theoretical bedrock on which the notion of operational flexibility rests. Second, changes in the input mix are unlikely to be systematically influenced by much other than changes in the relative prices of the inputs (suitably proxied here by bilateral industry-weighted real exchange rates). While changes in production technology or the intensity of research and development might also influence the input mix in a particular year, such changes are not likely to be as regular as, or to correlate with, changes in real exchange rates. Third, there is, at the present time, no good reason to believe that changes in the mix of inputs used by manufacturing MNEs cause changes in real exchange rates. Hence reverse causality is not an issue here. And fourth, other measures of operational flexibility, such as changes in the levels of MNEs' intrafirm trade, are, as standard empirical work in international trade shows, more influenced by changes in countries' income levels than by exchange rate changes. For all these reasons, a good way to explore multinational operational flexibility that is driven by relative price changes is to compare changes in the level of home content with changes in real exchange rates.

DEPENDENT VARIABLES. In the manner just described, we explore the sourcing and production-shifting responses to exchange rate changes exhibited by two sets of multinational affiliates in manufacturing industries: the Canadian, European, and Japanese manufacturing affiliates of MNEs headquartered in the United States; and the U.S. manufacturing affiliates of MNEs headquartered in Canada, Europe, and Japan.

The changes in home content are measures of "volume" rather than value. To calculate such changes in sales made abroad by U.S. MNEs' majority-owned foreign affiliates (MOFAs), let $V_0$ and $M_0$ be the period 0 value of foreign subsidiary sales and home imports, respectively.[27] The home content level in period 0 is simply $M_0/V_0$. In period 1, foreign subsidiary sales and imports are first deflated as follows: $V_1/(1 + I_1^f)$ and $M_1/(1 + I_1^\$)$, where $I_1^f$ is the industry-weighted change in producer prices in the host country, and $I_1^\$$ is the industry-weighted change in U.S. export prices. This adjustment removes pure price effects. Then, in order to remove currency translation effects, we convert back into national currencies all MOFA sales figures (which are stated in current U.S. dollars) and rescale these national currency figures back into U.S. dollars at period 0 nominal exchange rate. Stating $e$ in terms of foreign currency units per U.S. dollar, the home content level in period 1 is

(3-1)
$$\frac{[M_1]^*(1 + I_1^f)^*e_o}{[V_1]^*(1 + I_1^\$)^*e_1}.$$

Expanding $M_1$ and $V_1$, (3-1) can be rewritten as

(3-2)
$$\frac{[Q_1^{M*}P_0^\$(1 + I_1^\$)]^*(1 + I_1^f)^*e_0}{\left[Q_1^V *P_0^f(1 + I_1^f)* \dfrac{1}{e_1}\right]*(1 + I_1^\$)^*e_1},$$

where $Q_1^M$, $Q_1^V$ are the period-1 quantities and $P_0^\$$, $P_0^f$ the period-0 prices of home imports and sales made by the foreign subsidiary. Reducing terms, we are left with

(3-3)
$$\left[\frac{Q_1^M}{Q_1^V}\right]*\left[\frac{P_0^\$}{P_0^f}*e_0\right],$$

which is the period-1 home content share stated in period-0 real exchange rate units. Substituting notation, equation (3-3) can be expressed as $s_t*R$, where $s_t$ is the period $t$ home content share, and $R$ is the constant period-0 real exchange rate.

The dependent variable is then the change in this share over an interval of time, or $[(s_t*R) - (s_{t-k}*R)]/(s_{t-k}*R)$. This becomes $\Delta s_{t,t-k}/s_{t-k}$.[28] Notice that neither exchange rates nor prices remain in the dependent variable; they enter only on the right-hand side as components of changes in the real exchange rate.

Our calculations show that the U.S. content in sales made by U.S. MNEs' manufacturing affiliates in the Netherlands dropped from 10.85 percent in 1977 to 7.68 percent in 1985 and then went back up to 8.20 percent in 1994 (table 3-1). Over the same respective periods, the foreign content in sales made by the U.S. manufacturing affiliates of Netherlands MNEs went from 5.55 percent to 12.13 percent, and then to 9.51 percent.

COVERAGE AND SOURCES OF DATA. Data for estimating content levels come primarily from the BEA's annual surveys of U.S. MNEs' operations abroad and foreign MNEs' operations in the United

**Table 3-1.** *Estimated U.S. and Foreign Content in Sales in Manufacturing, 1977–94*

Percent

| Country | 1977 | 1982 | 1985 | 1989 | 1994 |
|---|---|---|---|---|---|
| *U.S.content in sales by majority-owned foreign affiliates of U.S. multinationals* | | | | | |
| Australia | 9.81 | 8.28 | 7.68 | 7.67 | 8.89 |
| Canada | 32.41 | 30.91 | 36.64 | 36.38 | 42.33 |
| France | 5.80 | 6.21 | 4.81 | 4.56 | 4.92 |
| Germany | 4.99 | 3.94 | 4.13 | 5.77 | 7.35 |
| Italy | 5.28 | 4.12 | 3.94 | 5.60 | 4.19 |
| Japan | 11.04 | 10.83 | 9.28 | 13.21 | 12.90 |
| Netherlands | 10.85 | 12.23 | 7.68 | 8.42 | 8.20 |
| Switzerland | 17.62 | 7.27 | 3.56 | 5.37 | 6.94 |
| United Kingdom | 5.51 | 5.80 | 5.45 | 6.54 | 8.91 |
| *Foreign content in sales by U.S. affiliates of foreign multinationals* | | | | | |
| Canada | 17.67 | 7.73 | 9.65 | 9.37 | 11.05 |
| France | 8.18 | 16.19 | 14.72 | 12.68 | 13.83 |
| Germany | 7.08 | 8.35 | 14.47 | 10.91 | 10.16 |
| Japan | 10.67 | 19.07 | 22.11 | 14.59 | 9.30 |
| Netherlands | 5.55 | 7.27 | 12.13 | 9.39 | 9.51 |
| Switzerland | 6.17 | 6.08 | 8.13 | 5.70 | 6.29 |
| United Kingdom | 8.84 | 7.49 | 8.81 | 6.30 | 7.59 |

Source: Authors' estimates; methodology and sources are described in the text.

States. The data for U.S. MNEs abroad cover the period 1982–94, supplemented with the BEA's 1977 benchmark survey, and the data for foreign operations in the United States cover 1977–94. The period 1977–94 encompasses at least one prolonged episode of dollar appreciation and one of depreciation (figure 3-1), along with other less pronounced shifts in exchange rates. As noted at the outset of this chapter, these large bidirectional movements in the independent variable provide a natural experiment setting for this analysis.

Exchange rate data are from the International Monetary Fund, *International Financial Statistics*. Producer prices are from the Organization for Economic Cooperation and Development, *Indicators of*

*Industrial Activity,* and U.S. import and export prices are from the international price program of the U.S. Bureau of Labor Statistics. Country coverage is determined by the relative importance of countries as homes or hosts of MNEs, and by the availability of data. We examine the production-shifting responses of U.S. MOFAs in Canada, France, Germany, Italy, the Netherlands, Switzerland, United Kingdom, Japan, and Australia; and the responses of the U.S. affiliates of Canadian, French, German, Netherlands, Swiss, British, and Japanese MNEs.

INDEPENDENT AND CONTROL VARIABLES. The key independent variable in this analysis is the percentage change in industry-weighted, bilateral, real exchange rates. These figures are based on changes in bilateral nominal exchange rates and in industry-specific producer prices in the United States and the partner countries in the study. For example, the real exchange rate used in the study of U.S. manufacturing affiliates in Germany will reflect changes in the nominal exchange rate between the dollar and the deutsche mark, and the sales-share weighted changes in relative producer prices in the various subindustries in which U.S. manufacturing MNEs participate in Germany.

Further, the increase in the intensity of international competition, the liberalization of trade and other regulations (which made the trans-shipment of intermediate and final goods more attractive and feasible), and advances in transportation and in telecommunications have possibly made it more important, easier, and less expensive for MNEs to coordinate their production networks and operate flexibly over the 1977–94 period. As a control for these developments, a time-trend variable is added in the relevant regressions. Also, country dummies, lagged changes in exchange rates, changes in R&D/sales ratios, and changes in capacity utilization are included in certain specifications. The base empirical specifications are stated in note a of tables 3-2, 3-3, and 3-4, which present the first set of regression results.

*Empirical Results*

Table 3-2 presents regression results, by exchange rate episode, both for foreign MNEs operating in the United States and for U.S. MNEs operating abroad. Because the regressions follow MNE responses over prolonged (four- to six-year) intervals, they allow sufficient time for the adjustment process and lessen the effects of "noise" in any particular year. The results are for the dollar appreciation episode (columns 1 and 4), the dollar depreciation episode (columns 2 and 5), and the post-1989 period (columns 3 and 6), during which the dollar appreciated against certain currencies but depreciated against others. Because BEA surveys of the foreign operations of U.S. MNEs are not available for the four years from 1978 to 1981, column 4 covers only the 1982–85 portion of the full (1979–85) dollar appreciation episode.

In table 3-2, the coefficients of changes in the real exchange rate are positive throughout and statistically significant in four of the six columns. Even in column 6 the exchange rate change coefficient takes a *t*-statistic that is just shy of the 10 percent level of statistical significance. The magnitudes of the coefficients accord well with estimates reported in the empirical trade literature.[29] The adjusted $R^2$s indicate that the parsimonious model (apart from column 4) has good explanatory power. The results imply that MNEs in the Triad countries operate flexibly and respond to changes in the real exchange rate by shifting sourcing and possibly production to locations favored by the changes.

More detailed analysis can be performed on the operations of U.S. affiliates of foreign MNEs, for which annual data are available continuously between 1977 and 1994. Table 3-3 presents the results of regressions explaining year-to-year changes in home content for these affiliates. The coefficients on the exchange rate change variables are statistically significant except in two cases (Canada and Switzerland) and accord with estimates reported in the trade

**Table 3-2. Regressions Explaining Changes over Multiyear Intervals in the Home-Content Levels in Sales by U.S. Affiliates of Foreign Multinationals and by Foreign Affiliates of U.S. Multinationals in Manufacturing, 1979–94[a]**

| Independent variable | Foreign MNEs' U.S. affiliates | | | U.S. MNEs' foreign affiliates | | |
|---|---|---|---|---|---|---|
| | Home currencies depreciating, 1979–85[b] | Home currencies appreciating, 1985–89 | Home currencies appreciating and depreciating 1989–94 | Dollar appreciating, 1982–85 | Dollar depreciating, 1985–89 | Dollar appreciating and depreciating, 1989–94[c] |
| | (1) | (2) | (3) | (4) | (5) | (6) |
| Constant | −60.80 (−0.99) | 14.28 (1.06) | 11.17 (1.66) | 0.21 (0.01) | −28.51 (−1.65) | 9.36 (1.45) |
| Change in real exchange rates | 2.80 (2.46)* | 1.53 (2.77)** | 1.52 (2.46)* | 1.11 (1.06) | 1.49 (3.19)** | 1.19 (1.89) |
| *Summary statistics* | | | | | | |
| Adjusted $R^2$ | 0.46 | 0.53 | 0.46 | 0.02 | 0.51 | 0.24 |
| Number of observations | 7 | 7 | 7 | 9 | 9 | 8 |

Source: Authors' estimates based on data in *USDIA*, various issues, and *Foreign Direct Investment in the U.S.*, various issues.

*Significant at 10 percent.

**Significant at 5 percent.

a. Model: %Δ in home content = α + β* %Δ in real exchange rate + ε; numbers in parentheses are t-statistics.

b. For Japan, the yen depreciation is measured from 1978.

c. Results shown are without Japan. With Japan, the coefficient on exchange rates is 0.48, with a t-statistic of 0.81.

Table 3-3. Regressions Explaining Year-to-Year Changes in Home-Content Levels in Sales by U.S. Affiliates of Canadian, European, and Japanese Multinationals in Manufacturing, 1977–94[a]

| | All foreign[b] | Canada | | France | | Germany | | Netherlands | Switzerland | United Kingdom | | Japan |
|---|---|---|---|---|---|---|---|---|---|---|---|---|
| Independent variable | (1) | (2) | (3)[c] | (4) | (5)[c] | (6) | (7)[c] | (8) | (9) | (10) | (11) | (12) |
| Constant | 2.05 (0.62) | -11.09 (-1.28) | -0.25 (-0.03) | 6.00 (0.47) | 15.35 (0.82) | 4.86 (0.73) | 3.97 (0.56) | 1.36 (0.16) | 5.29 (0.43) | -4.29 (-0.71) | -7.48 (-1.17) | 10.92 (1.86)* |
| Change in real exchange rates | 1.06 (7.49)*** | 1.61 (1.45) | 1.96 (2.25)** | 1.15 (2.09)* | 1.43 (2.24)** | 0.92 (3.59)*** | 0.99 (3.73)*** | 1.43 (4.00)*** | 0.62 (1.38) | 0.93 (3.50)*** | 0.86 (3.26)*** | 1.26 (5.23)*** |
| Time trend | 0.01 (0.04) | 0.91 (1.18) | 0.20 (0.28) | -0.11 (-0.10) | -0.91 (-0.55) | -0.20 (-0.34) | -0.14 (-0.21) | 0.27 (0.35) | -0.31 (-0.28) | 0.46 (0.85) | 0.63 (1.08) | -0.83 (-1.55) |
| Change in R&D/sales | | | -0.31 (-3.36)*** | | | | | | | | | |
| Change in capacity utilization | | | | | 3.91 (1.43) | | 0.83 (0.90) | | | | | |
| Summary statistics | | | | | | | | | | | | |
| Adjusted $R^2$ | 0.32 | 0.08 | 0.49 | 0.15 | 0.23 | 0.43 | 0.44 | 0.47 | 0.01 | 0.42 | 0.48 | 0.68 |
| Number of observations | 119 | 17 | 16 | 17 | 14 | 17 | 16 | 17 | 17 | 17 | 16 | 17 |

Source: Authors' estimates.
*Significant at 10 percent.
**Significant at 5 percent.
***Significant at 1 percent.
a. Model: %Δ in home content = $\alpha$ + $\beta$* %Δ in real exchange rate + $\gamma$* time trend + $\varepsilon$; numbers in parentheses are $t$-statistics.
b. Refers to the seven countries in the table.
c. Estimates are for 1977–93.

**Table 3-4.** *Exchange Rate Elasticities of Home Content for U.S. Affiliates of German, British, and Japanese Multinationals in Manufacturing, by Industry, 1977–94*[a]

| Industry | Country of headquarters | | |
|---|---|---|---|
| | Germany | United Kingdom | Japan |
| All manufacturing | 0.92*** | 0.93*** | 1.26*** |
| Food | −0.05 | 1.50*** | −1.70 |
| Chemicals | 0.21 | 1.26*** | 4.18** |
| Metals | 2.62*** | −2.47 | 0.41 |
| Machinery, except electrical | 0.80 | 0.17 | 2.29*** |
| Electrical machinery | 0.90 | 1.89** | 0.49 |
| Transportation | n.a. | −0.41** | n.a. |

Source: Authors' estimates.
n.a. Not available.
**Significant at 5 percent.
***Significant at 1 percent.
a. Model: %$\Delta$ in home content = $\alpha$ + $\beta$* %$\Delta$ in real exchange rate + $\gamma$* time trend + $\varepsilon$.

literature.[30] The adjusted $R^2$s appear reasonable. Interestingly, the coefficients on the time trend variable are neither consistently signed nor, in any instance, statistically significant. These results did not change when the time trend was run as an interaction term with changes in the exchange rate.

When the model in column 1 of table 3-3 was reestimated with country dummies, the results again remained unchanged. None of the country dummies were statistically significant. Likewise, when lagged changes in exchange rates were included in these regressions, they turned out to be neither large nor statistically significant. Since the data consist of annual figures, this result is not implausible (but see chapter 4 for further discussion of lags).

To investigate whether changes in R&D intensity explain movements in home content, the country regressions were rerun with changes in R&D/sales ratios added as a control variable. Only in the case of Canada (see table 3-3, column 3) was the variable itself statistically significant and did it noticeably alter the previous results. In this case, a change in the exchange rate turns statistically significant. For the United Kingdom (see table 3-3, column 11), the change in R&D/sales ratio is not statistically significant nor does it greatly alter the previous results. As for the other countries, the change in R&D intensity neither altered the previous results (that is, only exchange rate changes remained positive and significant) nor took on statistical significance itself. Results of regressions with changes in capacity utilization (to be discussed shortly) are shown in table 3-3, columns 5 and 7.

Regressions were also run at the industry level, but the results (table 3-4) need to be interpreted with caution because a good deal of data at the country-by-industry level were missing. The three countries chosen for the analysis (Germany, the United Kingdom, and Japan) were those for which reliable data were mostly available. The results here suggest, first, that all the industries with the exception of transportation have statistically significant and positive coefficients in at least one of the three cases presented. Chemicals turn out to be statistically significant in two cases. Because of large standard errors, the magnitude of the coefficients is not statistically different. The elasticities just for the United Kingdom seem to suggest that food, chemicals, and electrical machinery have larger than average coefficients (in relation to all manufacturing). But more complete and reliable data would be required to obtain more confident results.

## Discussion

The results just reviewed, however, provide compelling evidence that MNEs shift production systematically in response to real exchange rate changes, and that the vigor with which they do so is unaffected by the country in which they are headquartered. This picture is inconsistent with the flexibility-pessimism view. Given its emphasis on organizational factors, the pessimism hypothesis would lead one to expect sticky responses and (since MNEs from Europe, Japan, and the United States have historically been organized differently) marked national differences.[31] But we find little to differentiate the responsiveness of MNEs headquartered in the Triad countries in the sample. Consequently, the second hypothesis—that there are no noticeable responses—can be safely rejected.

This is not to say that organizational resistance stemming from a variety of sources is nonexistent in MNEs; rather, in the face of large movements in exchange rates (as witnessed during the 1980s), multinational managers—at headquarters or at affiliates, or possibly in both places—were able to perceive and exploit the opportunity provided by operational flexibility. Hence, in the context of operational flexibility, economic rationality appears to be a reasonable guide to MNE behavior.

The choice, then, lies between the flexibility-optimism and the flexibility-realism hypotheses. MNE direct costs and operating income provide some helpful clues (table 3-5). For MNEs operating in the industries we are exploring, direct costs account for a substantial proportion of total costs. Under the optimism hypothesis, as much as 10 to 20 percent of costs at the affected facility, even setting aside direct labor and overhead, ought to be "movable."[32] As table 3-1 shows, however, the actual shifts are not nearly as large. When, for example, the dollar depreciated by more than 40 percent in relation to the deutsche mark during 1985–89, the German affiliates of U.S. MNEs did raise the U.S. content in the products they sold, but the shift amounted to less than two percentage points, going from 4.13 percent to just 5.77 percent. Over the same period, the U.S. affiliates of German MNEs lowered their reliance on German content by less than four percentage points: it declined from 14.47 to just 10.91 percent. Such diminutive shifts in the input mix in the face of enormous changes in real exchange rates are noticeable for the other countries too. These relatively modest, but statistically significant, moves seem

**Table 3-5.** *Direct Costs and Operating Income for Selected Large Multinational Firms, 1992*[a]

| SIC code | Industry | Directly allocated costs as proportion of total[b] Average[d] | Range | Operating income[c] As a percentage of sales[d] | Per firm (millions of dollars)[d] |
|---|---|---|---|---|---|
| 20 | Food | 0.69 | 0.42–1.00 | 12 | 2,671 |
| 28 | Chemicals and allied products | 0.58 | 0.19–0.96 | 14 | 1,446 |
| 33, 34 | Primary and fabricated metals | 0.83 | 0.44–0.97 | 5 | 279 |
| 35 | Machinery, except electrical | 0.64 | 0.35–0.91 | 4 | 1,112 |
| 36 | Electric and electronic equipment | 0.73 | 0.38–0.97 | 9 | 2,916 |
| 371 | Automobiles | 0.83 | 0.48–0.97 | 3 | 2,258 |

Source: Authors' estimates based on data from Standard & Poor's *Compustat*, CD-ROM (December 1995). Estimates are based on figures for the 50 largest firms (sales basis) in each industry listed. Therefore, the data in the table pertain to a total of 300 firms. Invariably, multinational enterprises from the United States, Europe, and Japan constituted the vast majority of the 50 firms in each industry.

a. Direct cost ratios were in every case similar or larger in 1982.

b. Ratio is estimated by dividing the cost of goods sold into total costs. Cost of goods sold refers to directly allocated material, labor, and overhead. Total costs are computed as net sales minus operating income after depreciation.

c. Operating income is estimated as net sales minus the sum of cost of goods sold, selling, general and administrative expenses, and depreciation.

d. Figures are firm sales-weighted averages.

more consistent with the flexibility-realism perspective than with the flexibility-optimism perspective.

Of course, we would have greater confidence in arguing this point if we could rule out an obvious alternative explanation, namely, capacity limits. After all, flexibility optimists could argue that perhaps physical capacity limitations existed in the locations that were made more attractive by the exchange rate change, and this is what prevented larger responses. However, when change in capacity utilization (in the region in which expansion is warranted) is added as an independent variable to the regressions (table 3-3, columns 5 and 7), it neither changes the previous results nor turns out to be statistically significant.[33] Consequently, capacity limitations cannot explain the small responses just described. (Remember, too, that the global competition of the 1980s is widely associated with over- and not undercapacity.) Hence the flexibility-realism hypothesis—which sees strong ties between present MNE behavior and past strategies, whose effects often "linger for decades"—is probably the best choice.[34]

### Alternative Explanations

It is, of course, possible to suggest still other explanations for the empirical patterns observed. Three notable proposals revolve around the nature of the data, the floors and ceilings on home content, and the costs of switching.

FEW WINNERS, MISLEADING AVERAGES, AND POOR DATA. It may be that the perceptible, but small, MNE responses reported here are due to the fact that the BEA data we analyzed are only from industries or countries, not from firms. Consequently, the BEA data reflect aggregate firm behavior. In principle, if some multinationals operated very flexibly—indeed, as flexibly as the optimism view might predict—and others did not operate flexibly at all, the average pattern could come out looking like what we have described.

This is an important hypothesis to consider because the ability to operate flexibly no doubt varies among firms even within the same industry and country.[35] Still, misleading averages are not the likely answer. To begin with, one should not forget the widely recognized "follow-the-leader" behavior of MNEs.[36] Invariably engaged in small-numbers oligopolistic rivalry, these firms often study and imitate their opponents. Thus it is far from likely that a handful of MNEs would be operating exceptionally flexibly while rival firms lagged far behind. A search of the literature revealed no direct evidence (in the form of case studies or extensive business articles) to suggest that a few, let alone several, MNEs have pulled far ahead of the pack. Nevertheless, this view warrants closer examination and ought to be pursued in future research focused on the firm level.

As for the quality of the data, we see no serious problems such as measurement error because the variables used in this study are first-differenced (that is, measured in terms of changes, not levels). Furthermore, other researchers who have used the same BEA surveys have reported no significant errors or drawbacks in the data.[37] In fact, when the same data but a different methodology were used to examine employment substitution responses within U.S. MNEs, the results accorded well with the findings of this study.[38]

FLOORS AND CEILINGS ON HOME CONTENT. As already pointed out, the technology of production and "location-boundedness" of certain activities may, in principle, create floors and ceilings that home content is unable to penetrate. For instance, a critical or highly scale-intensive input may have to be fabricated in a single facility located at home owing to historical and market-size reasons. Certain activities (including distribution, sales, and service) may also have to remain local. If the MNE affiliate is operating near the floor or ceiling, it may not exhibit operational flexibility in response to appreciation (depreciation) in the home currency. This hypothesis is plausible and merits further development in future research. However, visual inspection of the response patterns does not reveal nonlinearities (predicted by this hypothesis) in the relationship between home content and real exchange rate changes. More important, the actual level of floors and ceilings will, to a great extent, be a function of previous investments in flexibility. Furthermore, one would expect floors and ceilings to be fixed in the short and medium run. Hence muted responses nine years (between 1985 and 1994) into a 30 to 40 percent dollar depreciation are more likely to be connected to search and switching costs.

CONVEX SEARCH AND SWITCHING COSTS. Flexibility is said to refer to "the cost, or possibility, of moving to various second period positions."[39] We have been arguing the "possibility" case thus far, but what of the case for costs? Seemingly obvious, this explanation would propose that switching costs are high and often convex: the more you switch, the more it costs per unit to switch. Under such circumstances, switching a little might be optimal, but switching a lot is not. Similarly, the search for new suppliers can be a difficult and lengthy process; and the related transaction costs may be high.

Although intuitively appealing and probably correct, this explanation puts the cart before the horse: it assumes search and switching costs are exogenous. But they should not be; in fact, as the flexibility realist would argue, the earlier and the greater the investments in operational flexibility, the lower the search and switching costs, and the less the convexity of those costs. In the end, search and switching costs merely reinforce the flexibility-realism view but do not constitute an alternative explanation. (We will have more to say on this in chapter 4.)

## Sourcing Responses of Japanese Multinationals

Another important question that merits attention here is whether multinationals from Japan behave differently. In the case of Japanese multinationals operating in the United States, foreign (that is, Japanese) content doubled between 1977 and 1985, when the dollar was appreciating, going from 10.67 to 22.11 percent. Subsequently, when the dollar dropped, the foreign content dropped, from 22.11 percent in 1985 to 14.59 percent in 1989, and then to 9.30 percent in 1994. Not surprisingly, our regression results (table 3-3, column 12) strongly indicate that the sourcing behavior of Japanese multinationals is responsive to exchange rate changes. Moreover, when we compare the sourcing responses of Japanese multinationals in the United States to, say, those of multinationals from the United Kingdom (whose industry mix of operations in the United States is similar to that of the Japanese multinationals there), we find no statistical differences.

Some observers have also suggested that an MNE's foreign vintage may have some bearing on home content: that is to say, the more recent a company's direct investment in a host country, the more the firm is likely to rely on home operations. This is a variant of the "liability of newness" argument.

We have tried to address this issue, at least in part, by including a time trend in our regressions. Indeed, the coefficient on the time trend variable for Japan (table 3-3, column 12) does take a negative sign (although it is statistically significant only at the 15 percent level). In order to explore the vintage explanation a little further, we estimated a vintage variable for inward direct investment stocks in the United States from Japan, Canada, and Europe. For instance, to estimate the vintage in 1994 of inward U.S. direct investment from Japan, we assigned an age to each year starting in 1950 (the earliest year for which we were able to gather data on the flow of foreign direct investment, FDI), and then we calculated a weighted age for the imputed FDI stock in 1994. Weights in the calculation are based on the size of the nominal dollar inflows in any year in relation to the nominal FDI stock that had cumulated by 1994, the reference year. Thus our procedure in estimating vintage in reference year $T$ (assuming $T > 1950$) can be expressed as:

$$\sum_{t=1950}^{T} \left[ \frac{Flow_t}{\sum\limits_{t=1950}^{T} Flow_t} * (T - t + 1) \right].$$

From our admittedly crude "vintage" estimates for seven developed countries (table 3-6), it seems that in 1977 Japan had the youngest vintage of the group (3.5 years), Canada had the oldest (9.4 years), and the average was 7.3 years. When the nominal inflow figures are adjusted by the U.S. GDP price deflator, older investments obtain larger weights, and the average vintage in 1977 rises to 9.4 years. What is striking, but consistent with the sizable cross-border FDI flows into the United States in the 1980s, is the youth

**Table 3-6.** *Estimated Vintage of Imputed "Stocks" of U.S. Inward Foreign Direct Investment from Selected Developed Countries, 1977–94*[a]

Vintage in years

| | *Year for which vintage is estimated* | | | | |
|---|---|---|---|---|---|
| *Home country* | *1977* | *1982* | *1985* | *1989* | *1994* |
| Canada | 9.4 | 8.0 | 8.6 | 8.8 | 10.3 |
| France | 4.1 | 4.5 | 6.7 | 5.1 | 6.0 |
| Germany | 4.8 | 4.9 | 5.6 | 5.9 | 7.1 |
| Japan | 3.5 | 3.9 | 4.4 | 3.8 | 6.9 |
| Netherlands | 7.1 | 4.8 | 6.2 | 6.7 | 9.9 |
| Switzerland | 8.0 | 7.6 | 6.7 | 6.3 | 8.3 |
| United Kingdom | 8.2 | 5.5 | 5.7 | 4.9 | 8.2 |
| *All seven home countries* | | | | | |
| Based on nominal inflows | 7.3 | 5.6 | 6.1 | 5.4 | 8.1 |
| Based on price-adjusted inflows | 9.4 | 7.9 | 8.5 | 7.5 | 10.2 |

Source: Authors' estimates; methodology and sources described in the text.

a. Except where stated, estimates are based on nominal FDI dollar inflows.

(5.4 years) of the imputed inward FDI stock in the United States at the end of the 1980s.

With the aid of these figures, we incorporated changes in vintage into our regression models (in table 3-3). Again, the dependent variable was the year-to-year change between 1977 and 1994 in the foreign-content level in sales made by the U.S. affiliates of foreign multinationals in manufacturing. The new results for Japan (table 3-7, column 10) compared with the results of the base model (see column 9), show no change in the magnitude or significance of the exchange rate coefficient. The time trend variable continues to be negative and borderline in significance. And the coefficient on the vintage change variable is positive but not statistically significant. Even when the model in column 10 is run without the time trend variable (not shown), the results do not change. Therefore, except to the extent that the coefficient on the time trend variable is negative, there appears to be little direct support for the vintage story in the regressions for Japan.

**Table 3-7. Regressions Explaining Year-to-Year Changes in Home-Content Levels in Sales by U.S. Affiliates of Foreign Multinationals in Manufacturing, 1977–94[a]**

| Independent variables | Seven foreign[b] (1) | (2) | Germany (3) | (4) | Netherlands (5) | (6) | United Kingdom (7) | (8) | Japan (9) | (10) |
|---|---|---|---|---|---|---|---|---|---|---|
| Constant | 2.05 (0.62) | 3.13 (0.95) | 4.86 (0.73) | 4.81 (0.84) | 1.36 (0.16) | 12.68 (1.31) | -4.29 (-0.71) | -4.15 (-0.51) | 10.92 (1.86)* | 11.69 (1.93)* |
| Change in real exchange rates | 1.06 (7.49)*** | 1.05 (7.50)*** | 0.92 (3.59)*** | 0.82 (3.67)*** | 1.43 (4.00)*** | 1.36 (4.15)*** | 0.93 (3.50)*** | 0.93 (3.37)*** | 1.26 (5.23)*** | 1.20 (4.75)*** |
| Time trend | 0.01 (0.04) | -0.16 (-0.53) | -0.20 (-0.34) | -0.35 (-0.69) | 0.27 (0.35) | -1.13 (-1.13) | 0.46 (0.85) | 0.45 (0.58) | -0.83 (-1.55) | -1.03 (-1.70) |
| Change in vintage of partner country's direct investment stock in the United States | ... | 0.31 (2.03)** | ... | 0.56 (2.42)** | ... | 1.19 (1.95)* | ... | 0.45 (0.03) | ... | 0.25 (0.75) |
| *Summary statistics* | | | | | | | | | | |
| Adjusted $R^2$ | 0.32 | 0.33 | 0.43 | 0.58 | 0.47 | 0.56 | 0.42 | 0.38 | 0.68 | 0.66 |
| Number of observations | 119 | 119 | 17 | 17 | 17 | 17 | 17 | 17 | 17 | 17 |

Source: Authors' estimates.
*Significant at 10 percent.
**Significant at 5 percent.
***Significant at 1 percent.
a. Model: %Δ in home content = $\alpha$ + $\beta$* %Δ in real exchange rate + $\gamma$* time trend + $\varepsilon$; numbers in parentheses are $t$-statistics.
b. Refers to Canada, France, Germany, Netherlands, Switzerland, United Kingdom, and Japan.

When we ran similar regressions for the other countries in the group, the exchange rate coefficient remained unchanged, but the vintage change variable (table 3-7, column 2) took a positive sign and was statistically significant. Recall that an increase in vintage means the inward FDI stock has grown older. If one assumes that the older the stock, the higher the U.S. content and the lower the foreign content, then the coefficient should have been negative, not positive.

This positive result might be explained as follows. Multinational firms anticipate a liability of foreignness and therefore are unlikely to make their investments into the United States (or any other foreign country) in one go. A firm wishing to establish, say, a $1 billion facility might bring in $200 million of that amount in the first year and then concentrate on deepening its links with qualified local labor and local suppliers. Once that objective was accomplished to its satisfaction, the firm would bring in the next $300 million, and it might once again seek to ratchet up its local value added. When further suitable business connections were established, say, in the subsequent year, the firm would bring in the remaining $500 million.

Over the three years, according to our estimation procedure, the vintage of the FDI stock would drop (because the bigger inflows are more recent), but the foreign content level in the firm's U.S. sales would drop off too. Such a model of progressive (as opposed to single-step) investment would generate (at least at the firm level) a positive coefficient on changes in vintage, as observed in table 3-8, column 2. (In such a model one would expect the time trend to take a negative trend, as it does in table 3-7, column 2.) Since the sample of firms in our database is not fixed and our empirical analysis is rather simple, we would not push this story too far.

Returning to the central question of this section, these and the previous results discussed in this chapter provide compelling evidence that Japanese multinationals respond at least as elastically to

**Table 3-8.** *Estimated U.S. Content in Sales by U.S. Multinationals' Majority-Owned Affiliates in Manufacturing, Seven Asian Economies, 1977–94*

Percent

| Country | Year | | | | |
|---------|------|------|------|------|------|
|         | 1977 | 1982 | 1985 | 1989 | 1994 |
| Hong Kong | 19.91 | 19.30 | 20.76 | 14.83 | ... |
| Malaysia | 37.10 | 54.88 | 40.18 | 28.56 | 14.13 |
| Philippines | 5.24 | 14.54 | 22.24 | 13.01 | 9.49 |
| Singapore | 18.52 | 29.89 | 21.13 | 17.83 | 13.44 |
| South Korea | 36.46 | 35.51 | 29.05 | 22.19 | 15.84 |
| Taiwan | 18.89 | 23.26 | 15.02 | 13.73 | ... |
| Thailand | 17.85 | 44.34 | 25.13 | 13.92 | 18.71 |

Source: Authors' estimates; methodology and sources are described in the text.

exchange rate changes as MNEs headquartered in Europe and the United States. With the appreciation of the yen since 1985, the U.S. affiliates of Japanese MNEs have relied far less on their home operations. This finding is consistent with conclusions reached in other empirical studies, which report that Japanese firms are not insensitive to price incentives, despite evidence of structural barriers.[40]

## U.S. Multinationals' Responses in Developing Countries

To determine whether and to what extent the U.S.-content patterns in sales made by the developing country affiliates of U.S. multinationals differ from those we saw in the developed countries, we calculated U.S. content in seven Asian economies for the period 1977–94: Hong Kong, Malaysia, the Philippines, Singapore, South Korea, Taiwan, and Thailand (see table 3-8).

Our methodology here differed from the developed country calculations in two respects: we used fixed industry weights (based on

1982 and 1989 data), rather than annually changing weights, to deflate U.S. manufacturing exports to, and the local manufacturing sales of, U.S. majority-owned foreign affiliates in those economies; and we used only the annual fourth-quarter export prices rather than an annual average of four quarterly price indexes. These changes saved us time and made it unnecessary to interpolate much missing data without, we are certain, affecting the quality of the results. Indeed, using this methodology to reestimate U.S. content levels in Australia, Canada, Europe, and Japan for the 1977–94 period, we found the pattern of movement in U.S. content levels to be virtually unchanged.

At least two patterns emerge in the developing economies: during the early 1980s U.S. content was substantially higher in developing economies than in the developed economies; and by 1994 U.S. content levels had dropped visibly. The first pattern is readily apparent in figure 3-4, which shows the levels in 1982 for U.S. MNE sales in twenty (developed and developing) economies. U.S. content hovers around 10 percent in the developed economies (except Canada) but is in the 15 to 50 percent range in the developing economies. Indeed, in a cross-sectional and pooled regression explaining U.S. content levels, the developing country dummy tends to be positive, large, and statistically significant (table 3-9, columns 1 and 5).

In an attempt to unpack the developing economy effect, we ran a regression on U.S.-content levels that included the following as independent variables: an estimated vintage of U.S. direct investment in the host country (estimates are presented in table 3-10); total GDP in the host country (as a proxy for local market size and potential for scale economies in local production); per capita GDP in the host country (as a proxy for level of capabilities and sophistication in the host economy); and a dummy variable for Canada. Since these are cross-sectional regressions, our earlier remarks about vintage effects should apply here (that is, the older the

**Figure 3-4.** *U.S. Content in Sales Made by U.S. Multinationals' Majority-Owned Foreign Affiliates in Manufacturing, Selected Economies, 1982*

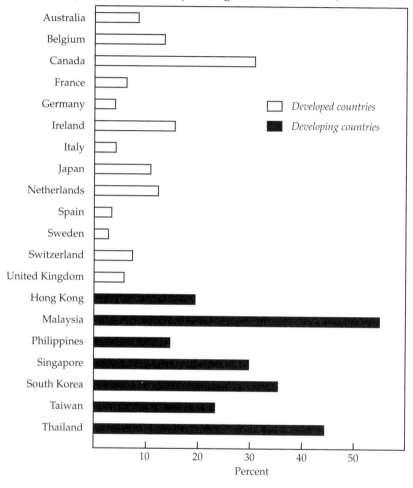

Source: Authors' estimates; methodology and data sources are described in the text.

vintage, the lower the U.S. content level). For obvious reasons, we also expect negative coefficients on the GDP and, especially, the per capita GDP variables.

As expected, the coefficient on the vintage variable turns out to be negative, and it is statistically significant throughout (table 3-9,

Table 3-9. *Cross-Sectional and Pooled Regressions Explaining U.S. Content Levels in Sales by Majority-Owned Foreign Affiliates of U.S. Multinationals, Selected Economies, 1977–94*[a]

| Independent variable | 1977 (1) | 1977 (2) | 1977 (3) | 1994[b] (4) | Pooled[b] (5) | Pooled[b] (6) |
|---|---|---|---|---|---|---|
| Constant | 7.54 (2.93)** | 41.05 (6.12)*** | 39.32 (3.19)*** | 26.16 (5.53)*** | 22.88 (4.60)*** | 37.20 (8.97)*** |
| Developing country dummy | 14.45 (3.62)*** | | 1.42 (0.17) | | 10.39 (3.72)*** | |
| Vintage of U.S. direct investment stock in host country | | −3.14 (−2.88)** | −3.11 (−2.69)** | −1.28 (−2.50)** | −1.74 (−3.21)*** | −2.13 (−4.05)*** |
| Host country GDP (billions of 1990 U.S. dollars) | | −0.01 (−1.64) | −0.01 (−1.33) | −0.002 (−1.36) | −0.002 (−0.52) | −0.004 (−1.48) |
| Host country per capita GDP (thousands of 1990 U.S. dollars) | | −0.04 (−0.11) | 0.03 (0.05) | −0.22 (−2.50)** | | −0.58 (−3.82)*** |

| | | | | | |
|---|---|---|---|---|---|
| Canada dummy | 21.34 | 33.57 | 33.37 | 33.33 | 32.17 | 33.55 |
| | (2.50)** | (3.78)*** | (3.56)*** | (9.46)*** | (7.09)*** | (7.34)*** |
| 1982 dummy | | | | | 3.27 | 3.10 |
| | | | | | (1.22) | (1.17) |
| 1989 dummy | | | | | 0.63 | 2.94 |
| | | | | | (0.22) | (1.11) |
| 1994 dummy | | | | | 0.09 | 3.19 |
| | | | | | (0.03) | (1.10) |
| *Summary statistics* | | | | | | |
| Adjusted $R^2$ | 0.46 | 0.64 | 0.61 | 0.91 | 0.61 | 0.61 |
| Number of observations | 18 | 16 | 16 | 13 | 58 | 58 |

Source: Authors' estimates.

** Significant at 5 percent.

*** Significant at 1 percent.

a. Numbers in parentheses are *t*-statistics. Regressions are based on available data for twenty economies: Australia, Belgium, Canada, France, Germany, Ireland, Italy, Japan, Netherlands, Spain, Sweden, Switzerland, the United Kingdom, Hong Kong, Malaysia, Philippines, Singapore, South Korea, Taiwan, and Thailand. Pooled regressions are based on cross-sectional observations for the years 1977, 1982, 1989, and 1994.

b. For reasons stated in the text, regression excludes Japan.

**Table 3-10.** *Estimated Vintage of Imputed "Stocks" of U.S. Outward Foreign Direct Investment, Selected Host Economies, 1977–94*[a]

Vintage in years

| Host country | Year for which vintage is estimated | | | | |
| --- | --- | --- | --- | --- | --- |
| | *1977* | *1982* | *1985* | *1989* | *1994* |
| Australia | 9.5 | 9.6 | 11.0 | 10.0 | 10.7 |
| Canada | 13.0 | 12.2 | 12.9 | 12.6 | 13.2 |
| France | 8.3 | 8.9 | 10.2 | 9.4 | 9.1 |
| Germany | 8.6 | 9.6 | 11.4 | 12.0 | 10.5 |
| Italy | 9.5 | 8.6 | 8.5 | 9.2 | 9.4 |
| Japan | 7.0 | 7.9 | 8.9 | 9.5 | 10.1 |
| Netherlands | 7.5 | 6.7 | 8.6 | 6.9 | 8.0 |
| Switzerland | 7.7 | 5.9 | 7.3 | 9.4 | 8.7 |
| United Kingdom | 7.7 | 7.4 | 8.2 | 8.1 | 8.1 |
| Weighted average | 9.6 | 9.2 | 10.1 | 9.9 | 9.7 |
| Hong Kong | 4.8 | 4.7 | 6.2 | 7.3 | 6.9 |
| Malaysia | 4.5 | 4.5 | 7.3 | 9.9 | 8.8 |
| Philippines | 10.7 | 10.3 | 11.9 | 15.1 | 11.5 |
| Singapore | 4.0 | 4.1 | 6.3 | 8.3 | 5.8 |
| South Korea | 5.1 | 5.9 | 7.4 | 7.4 | 8.5 |
| Taiwan | 6.3 | 5.3 | 6.1 | 5.9 | 6.7 |
| Thailand | 5.9 | 4.7 | 5.7 | 6.8 | 6.7 |
| Weighted average | 6.3 | 5.5 | 7.2 | 8.2 | 6.9 |

Source: Authors' estimates; methodology and sources described in the text.
a. Estimates are based on nominal U.S. FDI dollar outflows.

columns 2–6). This result is not surprising given that U.S. FDI in developing economies (except the Philippines) is of a substantially younger vintage than that in developed economies (see vintage estimates in table 3-10). Cross-sectionally, at least, the vintage variable takes the sign that we anticipate. Furthermore, although the coefficient on host country GDP is not statistically significant, it tends to be negative. (Japan is excluded in the models presented in columns 4–6 because U.S. content levels in Japan in 1994 were quite high in reaction to the depreciation of the dollar. When Japan is included in the 1994 regression, the coefficient on host country GDP takes a positive sign, whereas the other coefficients remain qualitatively unchanged.) The coefficient on per capita GDP—our proxy for country capabilities—is, as expected, negative throughout and statistically significant in columns 4 and 6.[41]

In sum, U.S. content levels are relatively high in developing economies, but they will probably decline as those economies grow. In fact, a decline is already under way (table 3-8). Between 1982 and 1994, the last year for which we had data, U.S. content levels in Asia dropped sharply. Regressions on changes in these content levels (shown in table 3-11) suggest that exchange rate changes by themselves have not played as significant a role in developing economies as in developed economies. This finding is not entirely surprising in the light of our earlier argument that the substitutability of geographic locations across developed economies is likely to be higher than across the United States and developing economies. Nevertheless, in the combined (developing and developed) regression models shown in table 3-11 (columns 3 and 4) and in figure 3-5, the exchange rate variable takes the correct sign and is statistically significant.

## Conclusion

Since the late 1970s the real exchange rate of the U.S. dollar has experienced some dramatic changes. Between the late 1970s and the mid-1980s the dollar rose sharply and then tumbled against major currencies (especially the Japanese yen) in the subsequent years. Using these exchange rate episodes as a natural test bed, we examined whether multinational enterprises respond by shifting their sourcing, and if they do so, whether their responsiveness differs by nationality of the parent firm. This work has provided compelling evidence of three main patterns of MNE behavior.

**Table 3-11.** *Regressions Explaining Changes over Multiyear Intervals in U.S. Content Levels in Sales by the Foreign Affiliates of U.S. Multinationals in Manufacturing, 1966–94*[a]

| Independent variable | Developed economies only[b] (1) | Developing economies only[c] (2) | Developing and developed economies (3) | Developing and developed economies (4) |
|---|---|---|---|---|
| Constant | 0.02 (0.26) | 0.02 (0.20) | 0.03 (0.47) | 0.03 (0.50) |
| Change in real exchange rates | 0.68 (3.95)*** | −0.53 (−0.94) | 0.57 (3.36)*** | 0.56 (3.24)*** |
| Developing economy dummy | . . . | . . . | . . . | −0.02 (−0.21) |
| *Summary statistics* | | | | |
| Adjusted $R^2$ | 0.19 | −0.00 | 0.11 | 0.09 |
| Number of observations | 63 | 29 | 92 | 92 |

Source: Authors' estimates.

*** Significant at 1 percent.

a. Model: %Δ in home content = α + β* %Δ in real exchange rate + ε; numbers in parentheses are *t*-statistics. Observations correspond to changes in the dependent and independent variables over the following time intervals: 1966–77, 1977–82, 1982–85, 1985–89, and 1989–94.

b. Includes Australia, Belgium, Canada, France, Germany, Ireland, Italy, Japan, Netherlands, Spain, Sweden, Switzerland, and the United Kingdom.

c. Includes Hong Kong, Malaysia, Philippines, Singapore, South Korea, Taiwan, and Thailand.

First, multinational firms shift production systematically in response to exchange rate changes, and the vigor with which they do so is unaffected by the country in which they are headquartered. This conclusion holds as well for Japanese multinationals operating in the United States. We are now able to confirm from a micro (firm-level) perspective something we have known from a macro perspective: exchange rate changes matter; and they influence behavior in a manner that aids the adjustment process.

Second, even in the face of the large exchange rate changes of the 1980s, MNEs' flexibility remained relatively modest. This finding lends credence to the view that MNEs do attempt to operate flexibly, but their ability to do so at present depends on strategies

**Figure 3-5.** *Change in Real Exchange Rates and U.S. Content Levels in Sales Made by Majority-Owned Foreign Affiliates of U.S. Multinationals, Selected Economies, 1985–89*[a]

Percentage change in U.S. content levels[b]

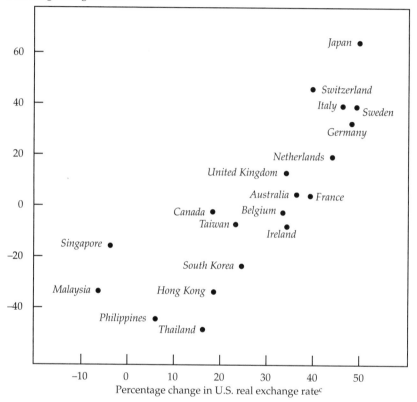

Percentage change in U.S. real exchange rate[c]

Source: Authors' estimates; methodology and sources described in the text.

a. Estimated elasticity is 1.42, with *t*-statistic: 5.58; intercept is –0.38, with *t*-statistic: –4.43; *n* is 19; adjusted $R^2$ is 0.63; *F*-statistic is 31.16.

b. The percentage change in U.S. content levels between 1985 and 1989 is the change in the share of U.S. content in sales made by MOFAs of U.S. multinational parents.

c. The U.S. real exchange rate is denominated as U.S. dollars per foreign currency unit; therefore positive (negative) changes between 1985 and 1989 represent a depreciation (appreciation) in the real exchange value of the dollar.

and actions taken in previous periods. Though obvious once stated, this view has been elided in the management literature. Instead, the tendency has been to assume that firms possess the requisite assets to operate flexibly, and then to concentrate on the ability of current managers to perceive and exploit latent advantages. The flexibility-realism hypothesis, however, does not question managers' ability in this regard but rather the starting assumption that the assets necessary for flexibility exist.

According to the flexibility-realism argument, regional mandates and bounded rationality (manifested in an inability to anticipate floating rates, sharp drops in tariffs, and sharp drops in the costs of coordination across distances) left multinational managers inattentive to operational flexibility in the period from 1950 to the early 1970s. Under the strong influence of this regional focus, their information sets and production capabilities were not very compatible across regions. Facing such congenital handicaps, multinational managers in the 1980s and early 1990s could achieve only modest success in their efforts to operate flexibly.

By highlighting the theoretical and empirical link between MNEs' previous actions and their current ability to operate flexibly, we have added some flesh to the widely held view that history matters. We have also helped substantiate that geographic locations (even across the developed nations of Europe, Japan, and North America) cannot be considered close substitutes, as the McKinnon-Mundell model supposes. Needless to say, this state of affairs may not persist. Indeed, the global strategies of multinational firms appear to be shifting toward a more integrated world economy, in which productive capacity will become more substitutable across borders.

Third, there is no evidence to support the hysteresis hypothesis in U.S. manufacturing. U.S. manufacturing capacity that had lost competitiveness during the early 1980s clearly regained its attractiveness during the second half of the 1980s, not only with U.S. firms but also with foreign firms.

As a next step, empirical research into multinational sourcing would do well to further examine the behavior of U.S. MNEs abroad. It should then proceed to the industry and the firm level (see our attempts at the latter in appendix B), where it may finally uncover the full picture of operational flexibility.

# Trade Responses of U.S. Multinationals | 4

A LONG-DEBATED QUESTION in the international business literature is whether the trade responses of multinational enterprises (MNEs) are stickier than arm's-length trade.[1] Views on the
issue fall in two camps: some believe intrafirm trade is, or ought to
be, no different from arm's-length trade;[2] others believe that such
trade is less responsive than arm's-length trade.[3] Those who predict
slow and small responses argue that intrafirm behavior reflects
hierarchical or command behavior and therefore is not likely to be
as sensitive to market considerations as arm's-length transactions.
The stand taken here is that MNEs ought to respond faster and
more vigorously, not because of special access to cross-border production capacity but because of information advantages arising out
of multinational operations.

This chapter draws heavily on Subramanian Rangan, "The Problem of Search and
Deliberation in International Exchange: Exploring Multinationals' Network Advan-
tages." That essay was awarded the 1998 Eldridge Haynes Prize by the Academy of
International Business.

This view, as we will show, can also shed light on macro patterns in trade responses. Three such patterns in particular have puzzled international economists. The first pertains to the long lags in trade responses to exchange rates. Even when exchange rate changes cause large and "permanent" shifts in relative prices, the geographic distribution of economic activity shifts slowly and hesitatingly. Established buyer-supplier relationships appear sticky, and switching is lagged. In contrast, when national incomes rise or fall, international trade adjusts both without long lag and more vigorously.

The second puzzling aspect of trade responses is the disproportionately large dampening effect that physical distance appears to have on bilateral trade. As many observers have noted, these effects seem far greater than transport costs alone could explain.

A third question of great interest, especially in recent times, pertains to the "home bias" in international trade and finance. This bias was clearly demonstrated in a study of the trade effects of the seemingly "innocuous" U.S.-Canada border, which looked like the prototypical case "if borders didn't matter."[4] But, after controlling for market size and "comparative advantage," the study found that in 1988, the year of the data, Canadians were twenty-two times more likely to trade with fellow Canadians than with persons *equally distant* but residing in the United States. Other studies have reported smaller quantitative effects, but they, too, point to a marked home bias in economic activity.[5]

Despite new bouts of theorizing on these questions, unifying and satisfactory explanations have eluded economists. One problem, some say, is that economists' macro models lack plausible micro foundations.[6] Whatever the trade model—whether of the Hecksher-Ohlin or Dixit-Stiglitz-Krugman variety—what appears to be missing, they contend, is "distance (and common polity, and common language, and common culture)." Further, a model in which such factors do play more of a role is probably one with "imperfect information, where familiarity declines rapidly with distance."[7]

The tentative hypothesis about MNE trade response to exchange rates put forth in this chapter offers some plausible micro foundations for the puzzling macro patterns just described. The hypothesis is built around a line of generalization that can be sketched as follows. In pursuing cross-border economic opportunities, firms engage in a process of *search* and *deliberation*. Search refers to acts performed in identifying potential exchange partners, and deliberation refers to acts performed in assessing their reliability and trustworthiness. Search grows more important as economic opportunities become more spatially dispersed, and deliberation grows more important the more costly it becomes to reverse the potential effects of allocative actions.

A number of institutions (such as organized markets and rating agencies) and innovations (such as advertising and warranties) have emerged to relieve the problems of search and deliberation and in many cases enable firms to pursue the economic opportunities they perceive. In the sphere of international trade and investment, however, such institutions and innovations do not exist or do not work well enough, leaving firms with insufficient information on which to base their decisions. Firms in those circumstances will exhibit a great deal of stickiness and lagged (or progressive) adjustment in responding to apparent cross-border economic opportunities. They will also turn to their business and social networks, because frequently those networks can help alleviate problems of search and deliberation and enable firms to uncover and exploit cross-border economic opportunities.

If this line of reasoning is valid, then, by extension, firms in the domain of international economic exchange that are embedded in well-elaborated social and business networks will tend to enjoy information advantages, and these advantages will enable them to adapt and respond more proficiently to new economic opportunities. Compared with their domestic counterparts, in particular, MNEs will tend to be embedded abroad in better-elaborated social networks. This latter characteristic ought to provide MNEs with information advantages (in addressing the problems of search and deliberation) that ought to generate speedier and more vigorous import responses.

The discussion here opens with the concepts of search and deliberation and the potential advantages in this regard gained from social networks. It then moves on to the contrasting trade responses to exchange rates among multinational and domestic enterprises. Subsequently, we discuss alternative explanations for our empirical findings, and then speculate about the micro-macro link between the problems of search and deliberation, the economic behavior of firms, and the puzzles mentioned at the outset. Our sense is that at their current pace, regionalization and globalization will tend to "shrink the globe" and dampen distance and border effects. At the same time, cross-border information discontinuities appear to be so profound at present that distance and (particularly) border effects in economic exchange will persist noticeably well into the future, although such discontinuities will be patched up as multinationals grow in number.

## The Problems of Search and Deliberation

As noted earlier, "search" is defined here as acts performed in identifying potential exchange partners. Firms engage in search when they sense that the action required to respond to a perceived economic opportunity or threat may lie outside the pattern of their current activities and exchange relationships. In general, the degree of difficulty experienced in search increases as potential exchange partners become more spread out. That is to say, search problems are a function of spatial dispersion. A corollary of this observation is that distance erodes economic exchange; "distance always shows up as a crucial determinant of trade flows."[8] Furthermore, although "shipping costs are quite small for most goods that can be shipped at all . . . trade falls off quite strongly with distance." It has also been suggested that distance may be a "proxy for more subtle transaction costs involving the difficulty of maintaining personal contact."[9]

"Deliberation" can be defined as the acts performed in assessing the reliability and trustworthiness of potential exchange partners. Like search, deliberation is an information-intensive process. However, it is aimed at reducing incomplete information about both the present and the future, especially the latter, whereas search is aimed at reducing incomplete information about the present. Deliberation is a nonissue if actors can be certain or nearly certain about the *quality* of what is to be exchanged and the *manner* in which exchange partners will discharge mutual obligations in the future. But in the absence of certainty, deliberation enters the picture, and it grows more important the more costly it becomes to reverse allocative actions or their effects. When actors view deliberation as important but problematic, they will tend to act reluctantly and progressively. In such circumstances, economic actions are unlikely to be influenced by relative prices alone.

Indeed, buyer-supplier relationships are often found to be sticky, and a good part of the explanation must lie beyond switching costs.[10] As in labor markets, assessing the reliability, timeliness, and capabilities of a new exchange partner is a process of discovery. As this process of discovery unfolds, the buying firm might be placing in circulation a stock of inferior products that upon discovery will be costly to recover and upgrade (as in the recall of vehicles fitted with defective components); developing dependencies with the new supplier that would be costly to reverse (as might happen when a firm turns over the management of its computer and information systems to an outside vendor); and closing off a return to previous exchange partners because the latter are likely to have tied up with other customers or have even exited the business altogether. These are some of the key sources of uninsurable costs that firms are bound to weigh before switching or settling upon exchange partners. The larger these factors loom, the more important it will be for firms to obtain reliable information about a potential exchange partner. If the requisite information cannot be assembled, however, firms are likely to forgo potential profit opportunities. Economic opportunities, like the proverbial dollar bill on the sidewalk, lie waiting to be picked up.

As already noted, whenever search and deliberation are problematic, business and social networks tend to assume greater significance in influencing economic actions and outcomes. Trade effects among immigrants provide a case in point. It has been suggested that the most important things immigrants bring with them are their links to their home country, for these ties can lower "transactions costs associated with obtaining foreign market information and establishing trade relationships." As empirical analysis demonstrates, social ties lead to a "direct increase in [trade] between the host and home countries."[11]

Such ties, sometimes described as "embeddedness," confer many information advantages on trade partners.[12] That is why search is often approached by simply calling and relying upon a known contact for a recommendation, rather than looking for objective information in government sources.[13] These advantages are especially important to deliberation. Because deliberation is to a large extent concerned with incomplete information about the future behavior of exchange partners, it is natural to look to past behavior for clues about future behavior. A firm's confidence in the reliability and trustworthiness of a potential exchange partner will tend to be much higher when the firm itself or someone it knows well has had "concrete personal relations" with the actor in question.[14]

## Search and Deliberation in International Trade

For most managers around the world, family and community ties, school and university ties, banking and boardroom ties, chamber of commerce and trade association ties, and ties to employers and co-workers tend to be local or national. As a result, it is more than distance, language, and culture that separates managers and firms from their counterparts in other nations. This would suggest that the problems of search and deliberation increase when economic exchange occurs across national borders.[15] It has been observed, for example, that "domestic vendor selection is more often a 'choice' situation. . . . International vendor selection, on the other hand, often is a 'search' situation, where the information processing load has a higher probability of exceeding the bound of human rationality."[16]

When interviewed, U.S. importers have stated that they "prefer long-term, stable, and direct relationships because [such relationships] 'make good business sense.'" Finding and evaluating new suppliers abroad is costly, buyer-supplier mutual learning (what we term co-specialization) is cumulative, and any "mutual obligation and trust develops incrementally." International buyers "are therefore reluctant to lose this advantage and start over with new partners."[17] Buyers whose allocative actions are costly to reverse will turn to the personal judgment of other buyers as their first source of information. Empirical observations of this nature and of price dispersion, lagged adjustment, and visibly modest price elasticities all suggest that the price mechanism does not work too well in international economic exchange.[18]

If international economic exchange is encumbered by the problems of search and deliberation, then actors embedded in well-elaborated cross-border networks should exhibit greater and speedier responses to international economic opportunities. This, in a nutshell, is why MNE trade responses to exchange rate changes can be expected to be speedier and more vigorous than arm's-length responses.

## Multinationals' Information Advantages

Multinational enterprises, by virtue of the fact that they operate in two or more countries, have the potential to be simultaneously embedded in two or more distinct social networks.[19] Most established multinationals already find themselves integrated into such networks through the concrete relations they have developed with local suppliers, customers, labor, and financial institutions. These external ties are supplemented to a lesser or greater degree by internal ties within the MNE (at least between the head office and the various foreign affiliates). Most U.S. MNE managers searching for external information, for example, reportedly turn to the corporation's own staff abroad.[20] Internal ties among managers in an MNE emerge from both formal and informal interaction, rotation, and other socialization processes.[21] This no doubt costly investment has long been thought to place the MNE in an advantageous position in comparison with nonmultinational enterprises.[22]

As pointed out in chapter 3, an MNE acquires this advantage when it locates and operates facilities in another advanced country, usually in response to a sizable demand for its products in that country (and the neighboring region). Routine operation of the foreign facility generates a set of business relationships and a continually replenished stock of information about actual prices, as well as the existence, location, and precise needs and capabilities of buyers and especially suppliers in that region. The pattern can be summarized as follows:

> When firm A starts to manufacture in country X, its subsidiary management, and perhaps its headquarters management, are exposed

to factor inputs and technologies that may differ in terms of type, quality, or cost from those previously encountered in the United States or elsewhere. In responding to this new matrix of factors, firm A may find that it can use new raw materials, or it may devise new manufacturing processes, or it may even uncover new product possibilities. Moreover, information about the discoveries can be transferred to other parts of A's organization.[23]

Although experiences are likely to vary greatly across firms and locations, most MNEs will tend to become structurally and relationally embedded in the host environment over time.

Now imagine that an MNE's home facility, facing a change in exchange rates, decides to explore the feasibility and economics of sourcing intermediate inputs from its foreign base. The home facility ought to be able to do this easily enough because the search and deliberation necessary to exploit the new economic opportunity are likely to be behind it. It will be much more difficult for the MNE's purely domestic counterparts to explore new opportunities, however, because the information and connections required to operate at home will be different from what is required for buying and selling abroad. Moreover, a local presence is frequently needed to ensure that the information exchanged is reliable and that transactions are settled under advantageous terms.[24]

This is not to say that nonmultinationals in arm's-length relationships will have no trade responses. On the contrary, given the growing intensity of competition, the large size of exchange rate changes over the last years, the fact that international trade existed long before anyone heard of multinational enterprises, and the empirical evidence from a voluminous literature, nonmultinationals can be fully expected to respond.[25] But, compared with their domestic counterparts, MNEs will tend to be embedded abroad in better-elaborated social networks. This characteristic of better structural and relational embeddedness ought to provide MNEs with information advantages in their search and deliberation activities, which should enable them to exhibit speedier and more vigorous import responses. The reasons for greater speed are obvious, and the reasons for greater vigor can be stated as follows. As argued earlier, deliberation problems tend to weaken a firm's willingness to substitute on the basis of price. In comparison with nonmultinational enterprises, MNEs, for reasons just laid out, face smaller deliberation problems. Other things equal, then, MNEs ought to exhibit higher exchange rate elasticities. Furthermore, the costs of search and deliberation can be considered additive to the purchase price.[26] Firms that face higher net prices will tend to trade smaller volumes than those that face lower net prices. By this logic, too, MNEs ought to exhibit higher exchange rate elasticities.

## Empirical Analysis

Using the United States as the focal country, the first step of the analysis is to pick an industry, partner country, and a time period, and then to examine the speed and elasticity with which U.S. imports in that industry, over that time period, and from that partner country respond to changes in the U.S. dollar's real exchange rate (in relation to the currency of that partner country). The next step is to compare the results with estimates of the same coefficients (in the same industry, partner country, and time period) for U.S. imports from U.S. multinationals that have operations in that partner country. Controlling for industry, country, and time period in this manner, we should, according to our propositions, observe that U.S. imports from MNEs exhibit statistically larger elasticities (that is, greater responses) and shorter lags (that is, speedier responses) in adapting to the common real exchange rate changes. Of course, any observed differences will be consistent with our search and deliberation story only if we can rule out MNE advantages that arise from other important sources, such as their size and sophistication. We will, therefore, attempt to control for these potentially confounding factors.

### Sources of Data and Coverage

Data used in the analysis come from three sources: the U.S. Department of Commerce, the Organization for Economic Cooperation and Development (OECD), and the International Monetary Fund (IMF). U.S. import data by country and by year were obtained from the Department of Commerce. Nominal exchange rates are from the IMF's *International Financial Statistics*. GDP data and industry- and country-specific producer prices (that are used to calculate industry-by-country-specific real exchange rates) are from the OECD's *Indicators of Industrial Activity*. Data on R&D expenditure are from the OECD's (1997) publication, *Research and Development Expenditure in Industry 1974–95*. Estimates of U.S. importers' employment size (used as an indicator of U.S. importers' firm size) are based on employment figures reported in volume 2 of the OECD (1997) publication, *Globalisation and Small and Medium Enterprises*. All data pertaining to U.S. multinationals are from annual surveys of the operations of U.S. multinationals and their foreign affiliates conducted by the U.S. Department of Commerce, Bureau of Economic Analysis (BEA). Since these latter data are available only on an annual basis, we rely on annual data in the analysis (using averages in the case of exchange rates and year-end data for all other variables).

Coverage is guided primarily by the availability of data (particularly on the operations of U.S. multinationals). Accordingly, the analysis concentrates on U.S. imports of manufactured goods in four industries between 1997 and 1994: food and related products, chemicals and allied products, nonelectrical machinery, and electric and electronic products. Imports are from nine countries: Australia, Canada, France, Germany, Italy, Japan, the Netherlands, Switzerland, and the United Kingdom. In 1994 U.S. imports in the four industries from these countries accounted for $123 billion, or a little more than a fifth of all U.S. manufacturing imports in that year. Depending on the specification estimated, the number of observations ranges from about 300 to 1,000. The lower limit is imposed by the lack of U.S. MNE data in many instances, especially for the period 1979–81, when the BEA conducted no surveys of U.S. MNEs' foreign operations.

Nevertheless, we gain an important advantage by focusing on MNEs with headquarters in the United States: by 1977, the first year covered in our study, these entities had already established operations in Europe, Canada, Australia, and Japan. In fact, between 1977 and 1994 the number of U.S. MNE parents in manufacturing actually declined slightly, from 1,842 to 1,543 (perhaps not inconsistent with the consolidation that had taken place domestically); and the number of foreign affiliates of these parents in the nine countries of interest declined slightly as well (mainly in Canada), from 11,771 to 11,189.[27] This relative stability in MNE affiliates abroad ought to mitigate concerns about shifts in the composition of the sample and about any potential simultaneity bias. Moreover, in the industries and countries we are studying (with the exception of Canada), less than 10 percent (typically less than 5 percent) of the output of U.S. firms' foreign affiliates is destined for shipment back to the United States, the point being that these affiliates were not set up as low-cost export platforms to serve the U.S. market. Rather, their priority from the start has been to serve local and regional markets abroad. This assures us that our sample data are not biased in favor of the hypotheses being explored.

Note, too, that although the MNE trade figures used in this study are the only set reported on a country-by-industry basis, they are primarily intrafirm trade data. Of the U.S. imports originated by U.S. MNEs' foreign affiliates, nearly 80 percent are shipped to the U.S. parent. As mentioned earlier, the commonly held view is that intrafirm trade ought to be no different from arm's-length trade, or it ought to be less responsive than arm's-length trade. Yet, since MNE intrafirm trade is likely to embody both internal and external ties and to benefit from the hypothesized information advantages, we expect intrafirm trade to be more responsive, ceteris paribus.

### Dependent Variable

Students of international trade have, in principle, a choice between focusing on imports or exports. Although empirical and policy-oriented research tends to concentrate on exports, in the present case imports are more suitable. The reason for this is straightforward: multinational enterprises are, in a sense, innately identified with exports and success in export markets.[28] Hence by sticking to imports we avoid biasing the results in favor of MNEs, as might be the case for MNE exports with a destination-market advantage. Purely domestic firms ought to be equally "at home" in the United States. Furthermore, since the United States is a more open economy than most, U.S. imports are likely to be a better register (than exports) of responses to new international economic opportunities. In other words, by selecting imports, variation in the dependent variable is likely to be enhanced.

Accordingly, the dependent variable used in the analysis is the log of U.S. imports from a particular country in a given industry and year. Ideally, we would want to state imports in volume terms. However, country- and industry-specific import prices are not available. We therefore rely on nominal import values. Other empirical studies have also taken this approach, noting that the magnitude of the reported elasticities will be greater in absolute terms.[29] In any event, since we will use nominal values for both MNEs and overall U.S. imports, our comparative analysis should not be thrown off in any way. Of course, transfer prices emerge as a potential issue, as discussed later in the chapter.

### Independent Variables

The first independent variable of interest is the real exchange rate (which is stated in terms of foreign currency units per U.S. dollar). We want to examine both the magnitude of the elasticity and the pattern of lags exhibited by U.S. MNEs and average U.S. importers in responding to the level of this independent variable. Whereas most studies tend to use exchange rates that are simply averaged across countries, we measure this variable in terms of specific country, industry, and year. In the case of U.S. imports of chemicals from Germany, for example, we construct the real exchange rate by adjusting the mark-dollar nominal rate to reflect producer prices in the U.S. and German chemical industries. In this manner, we construct an index of real exchange rates for the years 1977 through 1994 and use it in log terms in the analysis.

Another independent variable of interest is the interaction term between the real exchange rate and an MNE dummy variable. In regressions that pool MNE and average U.S. importer responses, we would expect the coefficient on this interaction term (MNE*exchange rate) to be positive and statistically significant. That is, after controlling for industry, year, partner country, and other variables stated below, MNEs, by virtue of their information advantages, ought to exhibit greater responsiveness to the level of the exchange rate than the average (nonmultinational) U.S. importer.

### Control Variables

Several control variables should be included in the analysis. First, we want to recognize that the decisions of U.S. firms to source inputs from abroad are influenced not only by exchange rates, but also by changes in the levels of their business activity. We therefore include as a control variable price-adjusted U.S. industry–specific GDP. This is an important variable in its own right, but here it gives us added insight, because, when their activity levels change, organizations (we assume) are simply adjusting quantities purchased up or down; they are not switching suppliers, and they do not have to search or deliberate.

According to our hypothesis, in the absence of search and deliberation, adjustment should be prompt and vigorous. Any lags on this variable should therefore be shorter than those observed on exchange rates. And, without ruling out other causes for this, the coefficient on this variable should be positive and larger than the coefficient on exchange rates.

Also important, to the extent that their greater experience, size, and sophistication enable MNEs to trade better, we should pick this up in an MNE*GDP interaction term. According to our theory, a positive coefficient on this interaction term would suggest the presence of advantages not related to superior networks and information. By implication, the MNE*GDP coefficient might serve as a sort of control against which we can compare the MNE*exchange rate coefficient (anticipating the latter to be larger than the former).

Separately, a firm size*exchange rate interaction term warrants inclusion because larger firms (read MNEs) can more readily justify the costs of hiring exchange rate specialists and persons proficient in foreign languages. Also, to the extent that search and switching costs are fixed, they will be more easily borne by large rather than small firms. Finally, larger firms may possess greater experience and hence expertise in executing the logistics required for successful international trade. On the other hand, it is well known that size can be a mixed blessing: large firms are more susceptible to "internal opportunism" and interdivisional "logrolling," both of which can impede flexibility and responsiveness.[30] Large firms are also more likely to be unionized, and this may influence their ability and willingness to substitute home content with imports. In addition, large size might confer scale economies that make short-run adjustments suboptimal. In any event, firm size is measured here by the average number of employees per U.S. firm in a given industry and year. Employment figures are not available for U.S. importers; estimates based on figures for U.S. exporters are used instead. For MNEs, the figures represent average MNE employment by industry. These data are also entered in log terms in the firm size*exchange rate interaction term. (Firm size is not entered by itself as an independent variable since it introduces perfect collinearity with the industry dummies in any given year and industry.)

A time trend is also entered in the regressions to account for advances in technology, the rise in capabilities abroad and the attendant rise in competition, and the greater liberalization in the world economy. To control for unobserved influences, dummy variables are included for eight of the nine countries and three of the four industries. In the regressions, then, the constant term stands for the omitted country and industry, which, in our case, will be the United Kingdom and machinery.

In some models (not described here), we included R&D/sales ratios as a control, because research intensity is believed to influence international trade, at least exports.[31] Since U.S. imports from country $X$ are country $X$'s exports to the United States, we controlled for foreign (that is, country $X$'s) industry-specific R&D/sales ratios. Since it usually takes time for research efforts to be reflected in new products and increased sales, we entered this variable on a two-year lagged basis. Including this variable did not change the results (and neither did alternative lag structures, including zero lags on R&D/sales).

*Model Estimation and Results*

Equations explaining U.S. imports are estimated as variations of the following specification:

$$\text{U.S. Imports}_{ijt} = \alpha_{ij} + \beta^*\text{U.S.GDP}_{it} + \gamma^*\text{Exch.Rate}_{ijt}$$
$$+ \ \delta^*\text{Importer Firm Size}_{it}{}^*\text{Exch.Rate}_{ijt} + \varepsilon^*\text{Time}_{t}$$
$$+ \ \zeta^*\text{Lagged Foreign R\&D/Sales}_{ijt}$$
$$+ \ \eta^*\text{MNE}_{ijt}{}^*\text{Exch.Rate}_{ijt} + \theta_{ijt}.$$

The subscripts $i$, $j$, and $t$, stand, respectively, for industry, country, and year. With the exception of the time trend (and the R&D/sales ratios) all variables are entered in natural logs. The coefficients on these latter variables therefore represent the elasticity of U.S. imports to a 1 percent increase in the respective independent variables. Pooling observations across industries and countries violates normal ordinary least squares (OLS) assumptions. To correct bias in parameter estimates, a least squares dummy variable approach is adopted. Such fixed-effects models constrain the coefficients on the independent variable to be the same across observations, but they allow unobserved cross-sectional heterogeneity to be captured in the different intercepts. This approach is well suited to panel data sets that are short and wide, as ours are.[32]

Consider, first, the models in columns 1 and 2 of table 4-1, which include the GDP, exchange rate, firm size, and the country and industry dummy variables. The first equation explains U.S. "overall" (meaning MNE *and* non-MNE related) imports from the nine countries in the four industries over the period 1977–94. The second equation explains U.S. imports originating from foreign affiliates of U.S. MNEs. In both equations, the coefficients on U.S. GDP are, as anticipated, positive, relatively large (around 2), and statistically significant. On the other hand, the coefficient on the (contemporaneous) real exchange rate is positive but not statistically significant

**Table 4-1. Regressions Explaining U.S. Manufacturing Imports in Food, Chemicals, Machinery, and Electrical Products, Selected Countries, 1977–94[a]**

| Independent variable | U.S. overall (1) | MNE (2) | U.S. overall (3) | MNE (4) | U.S. overall (5) | MNE (6) |
|---|---|---|---|---|---|---|
| Constant | -6.93*** (1.41) | -9.14*** (2.40) | -0.85 (2.60) | -2.59 (3.44) | -1.48 (2.64) | -3.79 (3.49) |
| U.S. industry GDP | 2.33*** (0.20) | 1.99*** (0.35) | 0.92* (0.50) | 0.54 (0.66) | 0.84* (0.50) | 0.45 (0.66) |
| Real exchange rate | 0.24 (0.37) | 2.60*** (0.91) | 0.07 (0.47) | 2.87*** (0.96) | 0.33 (0.52) | 3.42*** (1.00) |
| 1-year lagged real exchange rate | | | 0.69** (0.33) | 0.96* (0.52) | -0.10 (0.52) | 0.03 (0.72) |
| 2-year lagged real exchange rate | | | | | 0.74** (0.36) | 0.86** (0.47) |
| Time | | | 0.05*** (0.02) | 0.04 (0.03) | 0.05*** (0.02) | 0.04 (0.03) |

| | | | | | |
|---|---|---|---|---|---|
| Firm size*real exchange rate | 0.05 | −0.17** | −0.01 | −0.30*** | −0.01 | −0.31*** |
| | (0.05) | (0.08) | (0.05) | (0.09) | (0.06) | (0.08) |
| Chemical products | −0.53** | −0.36** | −0.24 | −0.14 | −0.27 | −0.12 |
| | (0.22) | (0.17) | (0.25) | (0.18) | (0.26) | (0.17) |
| Food products | −0.77*** | −0.77* | −0.76*** | −0.37 | −0.83*** | −0.33 |
| | (0.21) | (0.42) | (0.22) | (0.45) | (0.25) | (0.45) |
| Electrical products | −1.24*** | −1.15*** | −0.92*** | −0.70*** | −0.92*** | −0.68*** |
| | (0.15) | (0.22) | (0.18) | (0.24) | (0.19) | (0.24) |
| *Country dummies included?* | Yes | Yes | Yes | Yes | Yes | Yes |
| *Summary statistics* | | | | | | |
| Number of observations | 648 | 361 | 612 | 339 | 576 | 339 |
| Adjusted $R^2$ | 0.61 | 0.77 | 0.61 | 0.78 | 0.61 | 0.78 |
| F-statistic | 73.40*** | 87.60*** | 61.28*** | 73.60*** | 54.42*** | 69.98*** |

Source: Authors' estimates.
*Significant at 10 percent.
**Significant at 5 percent.
***Significant at 1 percent.

a. Numbers in parentheses are *t*-statistics. Regressions are based on annual data . All variables (except the time trend and the country and industry dummies) are entered in their natural logs. The dependent variable is U.S. industry-country-year-specific import values. Exchange rates are also industry-country-year-specific. U.S. GDP is industry and year specific. Firm size is measured in terms of average employees per firm in the United States and is industry and year specific. Regressions cover nine U.S. trade partners: Australia, Canada, France, Germany, Italy, Japan, Netherlands, Switzerland, and the United Kingdom.

for U.S. overall imports; for MNE imports, however, this coefficient is positive, significant, and larger than the coefficient on the GDP variable. When a time trend is added to these models (not shown), the pattern of the exchange rate coefficients remains unchanged. Not surprisingly, the time trend cancels out much of the effect associated with the rise in GDP. As indicated by their adjusted $R$-squares—of 0.61 and 0.77—these models explain a significant amount of the variation in the dependent variable.

The models in the other columns in table 4-1 explore the question of comparative speed of adjustment. The results in those columns clearly suggest that MNEs exhibit speedier responses. Consider the two models in columns 3 and 4 of table 4-1. Both contain the contemporaneous and one-year lagged exchange rates. The one-year lagged exchange rate coefficient for U.S. overall imports now assumes statistical significance. This is also the case for MNE imports, although contemporaneous exchange rates continue to be large and statistically significant. When two-year lagged exchange rates are added (in columns 5 and 6 of table 4-1), their coefficients assume significance for both U.S. overall and MNE imports. However, the sum of the exchange rate coefficients shows a marked difference between U.S. overall and MNE imports: for the former, their sum is 0.97; for the latter, it is 4.31. (When a lagged GDP term was added to the models in columns 5 and 6 of table 4-1, it did not take on a statistically significant coefficient.)

In table 4-2, we pool the overall and MNE-only observations and estimate regressions with interaction terms between the MNE dummy variable and the price and activity variables; we also explore the robustness of our results by running regressions on selected subsamples of the available data. First, note that the MNE*real exchange rate interaction term is positive and statistically significant in all the models shown in table 4-2. That is, MNEs with operations in the partner country exhibit a greater responsiveness to the level of the exchange rate than the average U.S.

importer does. Also, in this pooled sample (see column 1, for instance), the coefficient on the contemporaneous exchange rate assumes statistical significance. The coefficients on the GDP are also significant and much larger (in the absence of the time trend), and the adjusted $R$-square for the model in column 1 (0.73) is quite satisfactory.

Note that in many of the industry-country-years, especially for MNEs, import values are small. Upon inspection, we discovered that of the nine countries in the study, three—Australia, Italy, and Switzerland—had fragmentary and very small trade figures. To examine whether these were affecting the results, we decided to run a regression excluding Australia, Italy, and Switzerland, following which we found the MNE*exchange rate coefficient still statistically significant and higher in magnitude (table 4-1, column 2).

Next, in order to explore MNE size and sophistication as sources of superior MNE adjustment, we included an MNE*GDP interaction variable to the model just reviewed. As column 3 of table 4-2 shows, the MNE*GDP interaction term is positive and statistically significant. This finding is consistent with the view that MNEs enjoy adjustment advantages that might derive from greater international experience and superior communication and logistics capabilities. Yet the coefficient on the MNE*exchange rate interaction term is much larger than that on MNE*GDP (2.24 compared to 0.51). Furthermore, the appropriate $t$- and $F$-tests based on restricted and unrestricted regressions (not shown) indicate that the coefficients are statistically different. Running the model shown in column 3 with all available observations (see results in column 4 of table 4-2) weakens the difference between the two coefficients but does not alter the basic finding. (The same holds true for specifications that exclude the firm size*exchange rate interaction term).

In exploring the effects over time (table 4-3), we attempted to determine whether MNEs' information advantages were

**Table 4-2.** *Pooled Regressions Explaining U.S. Manufacturing Imports in Food, Chemicals, Machinery, and Electrical Products, Selected Countries, 1977–94*[a]

| | U.S. overall and MNE pooled | | | |
|---|---|---|---|---|
| Independent variable | All available observations (1) | Without Australia, Italy, and Switzerland (2) | Without Australia, Italy, and Switzerland (3) | All available observations (4) |
| U.S. industry GDP | 2.16*** (0.18) | 2.39*** (0.19) | 2.23*** (0.21) | 1.96*** (0.19) |
| Real exchange rate | 0.65** (0.33) | 0.79** (0.35) | 0.72** (0.35) | 0.57* (0.33) |
| Firm size*real exchange rate | −0.05 (0.03) | −0.06* (0.04) | −0.06 (0.04) | −0.04 (0.03) |
| MNE | −7.53*** (1.68) | −10.96*** (1.81) | −14.34*** (2.67) | −11.83*** (2.48) |
| MNE*real exchange rate | 1.23*** (0.39) | 2.09*** (0.42) | 2.24*** (0.43) | 1.42*** (0.40) |
| MNE*U.S. industry GDP | | | 0.51* (0.30) | 0.65** (0.28) |
| *Country and industry dummies included?* | Yes | Yes | Yes | Yes |
| *Summary statistics* | | | | |
| Number of observations | 1,009 | 685 | 685 | 1,009 |
| Adjusted $R^2$ | 0.73 | 0.73 | 0.73 | 0.73 |
| F-statistic | 172.28*** | 141.45*** | 131.94*** | 163.22*** |

Source: Authors' estimates.
*Significant at 10 percent.
**Significant at 5 percent.
***Significant at 1 percent.
a. Numbers in parentheses are *t*-statistics.

becoming more visible over time. Given that trade has been significantly liberalized over the past two decades, one might expect multinationals to have made better use of their information advantages over this time frame and to have grown more responsive.

**Table 4-3.** *Time Effects in Pooled Regressions Explaining U.S. Manufacturing Imports in Food, Chemicals, Machinery, and Electrical Products, Selected Countries, 1977–94*[a]

| Independent variable | U.S. overall and MNE pooled | | | |
|---|---|---|---|---|
| | *(1)* | *(2)* | *(3)* | *(4)* |
| U.S. industry GDP | 1.06*** | 0.95** | 1.01** | 0.92** |
| | (0.41) | (0.42) | (0.41) | (0.42) |
| Real exchange rate | 0.78** | 0.77** | 0.14 | 0.21 |
| | (0.33) | (0.33) | (0.46) | (0.47) |
| Firm size*real exchange | −0.07** | −0.07** | −0.07** | −0.07** |
| | (0.04) | (0.04) | (0.04) | 0.04) |
| Time | 0.05** | 0.05*** | −0.28* | −0.24 |
| | (0.02) | (0.02) | (0.17) | (0.17) |
| MNE | −7.91*** | −8.81*** | −7.41*** | −8.24*** |
| | (1.68) | (1.75) | (1.70) | (1.78) |
| MNE*real exchange rate | 1.37*** | 1.50*** | 1.26*** | 1.39*** |
| | (0.39) | (0.40) | (0.40) | (0.40) |
| MNE*real exchange rate*time | . . . | 0.01* | . . . | 0.01 |
| | | (0.00) | | (0.00) |
| Real exchange rate*time | . . . | . . . | 0.08** | 0.07* |
| | | | (0.04) | (0.04) |
| *Country and industry* dummies included? | Yes | Yes | Yes | Yes |
| *Summary statistics* | | | | |
| Number of observations | 1,009 | 1,009 | 1,009 | 1,009 |
| Adjusted $R^2$ | 0.73 | 0.73 | 0.74 | 0.73 |
| *F*-statistic | 163.90*** | 155.33*** | 155.45*** | 147.59*** |

Source: Authors' estimates.
*Significant at 10 percent.
**Significant at 5 percent.
***Significant at 1 percent.
a. Numbers in parentheses are *t*-statistics.

As the results in column 2 of table 4-3 show (see, in particular, the coefficient on MNE*real exchange rate*time), there is some support, albeit mild, for this view.

Since technology has advanced and "selection pressures" have in all likelihood ratcheted up over the past twenty years, it would also appear that, notwithstanding search and deliberation problems, the relative price (that is, exchange rate) responsiveness of all firms ought to have trended up. This supposition, too, is supported by the positive and statistically significant coefficient on the real exchange rate*time interaction term in column 3 of table 4-3. Running a model with both interaction terms (see column 4) maintained the results but reduced to 13 percent the significance of the coefficient on the MNE*real exchange rate*time interaction term.

In industry-by-industry regressions (not reported here), the MNE*exchange rate interaction term was positive for all four industries and statistically significant in three (machinery being the exception).[33] In order to check whether the search and deliberation story holds even in the absence of MNE-related data, we ran regressions using only overall U.S. import data. Reasoning that search and deliberation ought to be relatively easier for U.S. importers when they have to switch away from foreign suppliers back to U.S. suppliers, we examined whether the exchange rate coefficient was larger during dollar depreciations (say, during the 1986–90 period) than dollar appreciations (say, during the 1979–85 period). Not only was the contemporaneous exchange rate coefficient larger during depreciations (1.51 compared to 0.43 during appreciations), but it was also statistically significant at the 5 percent level. (The other coefficients took predictable values.)[34]

## Discussion

Our empirical results clearly indicate that intrafirm trade is not stickier than arm's-length trade. In fact, consistent with our arguments about MNEs' information advantages in dealing with the problems of search and deliberation, the results indicate that even in the case of imports MNEs exhibit speedier and more vigorous responses to changes in real exchange rates.

It is true that MNEs tend to enjoy internalization and experience advantages. Indeed, we found that the MNE*GDP coefficient took positive and significant values. But we also found that the

MNE*exchange rate interaction coefficient took much larger values, and this would support our contention that problematic search and deliberation and MNEs' information advantages are key explanators here. In addition, the average firm size*exchange rate variable took either a statistically insignificant or a significant but negative coefficient. This might be explained by the presence of scale economies, and it is not inconsistent with the view expressed in a recent OECD study on globalization: "Size does hold some importance, especially in successfully taking the first steps to internationalisation, but once there, it does not seem to matter much. . . . [S]maller size can often be an advantage."[35]

Of course, the internalized trade issue does raise the question of transfer prices. Intrafirm MNE transactions are typically made at internal transfer prices and internal exchange rates that tend to be rigid.[36] But if transfer prices remain stable in the currency of the originating country, and if company internal exchange rates lag behind actual exchange rates (say, because of the presence of currency hedge contracts), then, ceteris paribus, MNE import values will register smaller, not bigger, changes. (In fact, in our data, the simple correlation coefficient between MNE imports and exchange rates is close to zero.) MNE transfer pricing practices cannot therefore account for our findings. Indeed, they would strengthen our findings and explanation.

Two alternative explanations also merit discussion. First, we have not included capacity in our regressions in this chapter. But if capacity were important, it ought to be manifested in lags on income effects.[37] Since this is not the case here, we can rule out capacity as a key explanatory variable. Second, one might argue that although capacity constraints may not play a role, multinationals might have more *compatible* capacity across geographies and therefore be able to exploit relative price differences better. But recall that when we explored this question in the context of MNEs' foreign sourcing (in chapter 3), we concluded that owing to their historical local-for-local strategies, MNEs did not (during this period) appear to enjoy a high degree of cross-border compatibility in their production capacity. Last, but not least, a growing body of empirical work (based on data unrelated to the MNE trade figures we have used) is also reporting findings that are consistent with our emphasis on the role and advantages of business networks in international trade.[38]

With regard to the puzzling macro patterns mentioned earlier, we have suggested that search and deliberation problems are responsible for the lags and progressiveness in trade responses to exchange rates. Distance effects, over and beyond those explained by trade costs, are likely to be a manifestation of search problems. In other words, distance tends to make the search for potential exchange partners more cumbersome. The presence of organized markets is likely to mitigate those problems. By implication, distance ought to dampen more trade in goods (such as differentiated manufactures) that are not offered on organized exchanges. Physical distance is also likely to have declined in importance over the past couple of decades, since search has probably become easier and less expensive over this period.[39]

On the question of border effects (or home bias), we conclude that they are primarily a function of deliberation problems (or, contrariwise, a manifestation of a familiarity bias). Now if it were true, as would seem plausible, that trade in differentiated products represents economic action that is more costly to reverse than trade in commodities, then network effects ought to be relatively greater for differentiated products.[40]

A last piece of interesting evidence on these matters appears in a European Commission survey conducted in 1995 to assess the effect on company strategies of the EC '92 Single European Market initiative. In response to questions on their intra-European sourcing strategies, the vast majority of the (13,500) firms surveyed did not view the removal of intra-European border barriers (except in the

**Table 4-4.** *European Single Market's Importance in the Development of Firm Strategy*

Percent

| Purchase from other EU markets | Enterprises expressing opinion | | | | Enterprises expressing opinion, weighted by number of salaried employees | | | |
|---|---|---|---|---|---|---|---|---|
| | Very important | Quite important | Not important | Don't know | Very important | Quite important | Not important | Don't know |
| Raw materials | 10 | 24 | 48 | 19 | 11 | 31 | 45 | 13 |
| Components | 7 | 18 | 52 | 24 | 8 | 25 | 51 | 16 |
| Business services | 2 | 7 | 60 | 31 | 2 | 11 | 65 | 22 |
| Financial services | 1 | 6 | 58 | 35 | 2 | 10 | 62 | 25 |

Source: The European Commission, *The Single Market Review: Results of the Business Survey* (Luxembourg: Office for Official Publications of the European Communities, 1997), table EUR M.3, p. 23.

purchase of raw materials) as important to their sourcing strategies (see table 4-4). The figures under "very important" and "quite important" decline predictably as they go from raw materials, to components, to business services, to financial services. This pattern is roughly what one would expect if one believed that the importance of deliberation rises, as we believe it does, when one goes from raw materials to components to services. To be sure, if the survey is repeated a few years hence, the percentage of respondents falling under the "very important" and "quite important" columns would in all likelihood increase, but the declining pattern across the rows is likely to persist.

## Conclusion

When a firm has difficulty identifying and assessing potential exchange partners, it may well consider the available information too insufficient to pursue apparent economic opportunities. Problems of search and deliberation tend to become salient when economic opportunities are dispersed spatially or when economic actions or their effects are perceived as being costly to reverse.

Brought into the international setting, these simple ideas can help explain why parts of the global economy (such as currency markets) appear extremely volatile and responsive, whereas other parts (such as trade in manufactured goods) exhibit visible stickiness and lagged adjustment. Drawing on the preceding discussion, it is possible to propose relative positions on a search-deliberation frame for the major types of economic activity that span national borders (figure 4-1). If distance is a proxy for search problems and borders are a proxy for deliberation problems, then one would expect short lags and relatively small distance effects in portfolio investment, for example. However, international portfolio investments would be expected to exhibit large border (or home bias)

**Figure 4-1.** *Schematic Mapping of Selected Areas of International Economic Activity against Search and Deliberation Problems*

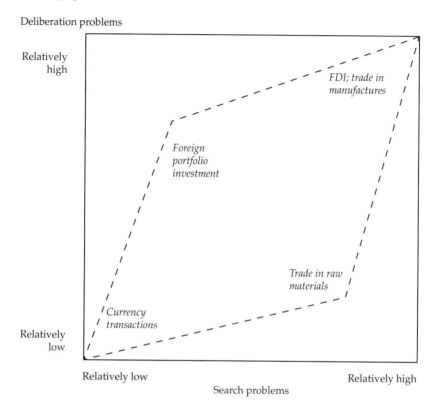

effects. Foreign direct investment (FDI), on the other hand, is to portfolio investment what trade in differentiated products is to trade in commodities.[41]

In the future, of course, search and deliberation problems are bound to subside somewhat, though perhaps not rapidly, as the technology of the Internet spreads further afield. As a result, distance effects will more closely reflect transport costs. A protracted period of trade and investment liberalization accompanied by a rising multinationalization of firms is also likely to temper cross-border deliberation problems, but again the change will not be rapid or dramatic. In other words, we expect border effects and the home bias to diminish in the future, but not to disappear. National (and regional) markets will probably remain segmented in the foreseeable future. And with the exception of standardized goods, firms will continue to be able to price to market. Therefore, above-normal price dispersion is likely to persist. After all, in most markets, trust and price will surely remain complements rather than turn into substitutes.

# Illustrative Models of International Pricing | A

IN INTERNATIONAL EXPORT MARKETS, the battle on behalf of the United States is fought mainly by large multinational enterprises. Like most firms, these entities tend to be preoccupied with profitability, market share, and stability. Small numbers, sharp rivalries, and uncertainty all go to make up the setting in which they operate.[1] In circumstances as complex as these, what constitutes an "optimal" response to exchange rate changes is likely to vary from firm to firm, depending on such factors as how committed a firm is to a particular foreign market, what impact it believes its performance in that market will have on its positions elsewhere, what future prospects this market or customer holds, how deep the firm's pockets are, what level of tolerance it has for sustaining losses, whether it sees an opportunity and wants to drive a rival out of the market, or whether it merely wants to signal that it has the power to do so but in return for cooperative behavior will not, and so on.

But this line of thinking runs the grave risk of "framing hypotheses that explain everything but predict nothing."[2] A more fruitful approach would be to consider the set of factors that might link exchange rate changes to foreign price changes in a systematic manner. That set includes the ability of producers to separate markets, their perceptions about the nature of demand, their cost functions, their beliefs about the likely reactions of rivals, their assessment of the importance of current market share in determining future profits, and their expectations about the future course of exchange rates.

Though not exhaustive, this list covers what is likely to be important. The factors it identifies are taken up here one or two at a time in a series of simple models. The viewpoint throughout is that of a U.S. producer serving two markets, the home market and the market abroad. The United States will be considered the home or domestic market and the dollar will be considered the home currency.

## Illustrative Models of Pricing Responses to Exchange Rate Changes

Arbitrage holds a special place in international economics because it determines whether producers can set, net of tariffs and transport costs, separate prices at home and abroad. Presumably, producers who have the ability to do so have more latitude in responding to exchange rate changes.

But what is the optimal course of action for producers who are constrained by the pressures of arbitrage to set uniform world prices? Should they maintain their world dollar prices and let their foreign currency prices change in full proportion to exchange rate changes? That is, does a high degree of arbitrage, in general, imply a high degree of pass-through? And in the extreme, does complete spatial arbitrage imply complete pass-through? Could the "openness" of U.S. markets and the ensuing pressures of arbitrage explain the behavior of U.S. export prices?

*The Ability to Separate Markets, the Elasticity of Demand,*
*and the Nature of Costs*

To isolate the pass-through effects of spatial arbitrage, we defer dynamic effects until later and consider the simple case of a U.S. producer who makes a specialized semiconductor device for sale at home and abroad. Manufacture of the device calls for such technical sophistication that the U.S. producer has a world monopoly on this product. (The assumption of monopoly is not necessary; it is made only to emphasize that the producer acts as a price setter. The case of oligopoly is considered later. The case of perfect competition is analyzed graphically in figure A-1.)

Assume that for a variety of reasons, including the high ratio of value to weight for this device, spatial arbitrage is complete. As a result, the producer is constrained by the "law of one price." This constraint is commonly written as

(A1) $$p_i = e p_i^*,$$

where $p_i$ is the dollar price of $i$, the semiconductor device, in the United States, $p_i^*$ is the foreign currency price charged abroad, and $e$ is the exchange rate in dollars per unit of foreign currency.[3]

Under these assumptions, the U.S. producer's profit maximizing uniform world dollar price for the device is given by:

(A2) $$p_i = \left( \frac{\eta_{us} \cdot \dfrac{q}{Q} + \eta_f \dfrac{q^*}{Q}}{\eta_{us} \cdot \dfrac{q}{Q} + \eta_f \dfrac{q^*}{Q} - 1} \right) c'(Q),$$

where the first term represents a markup and the second, $c'(Q)$, is the dollar marginal cost for the firm at output $Q$. The $\eta$s are the elas-

**Figure A-1.** *Exchange Rate Pass-Through under Perfect Competition and Complete Spatial Arbitrage*

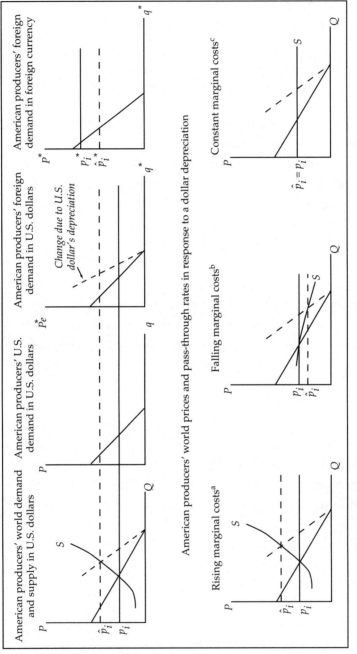

American producers' world prices and pass-through rates in response to a dollar depreciation

a. Pass-through incomplete: $|dp_i^*/p_i^*| < |de/e|$.
b. Pass-through more than complete: $|dp_i^*/p_i^*| > |de/e|$.
b. Pass-through just complete: $|dp_i^*/p_i^*| = |de/e|$.

ticities of demand in the U.S. and foreign market, and $q/Q$ and $q^*/Q$ are the respective shares of world sales achieved in the United States and foreign market. The price in foreign currency terms, $p_i^*$, will just be $p_i/e$. This much is straightforward.

It is also straightforward to see that under $p_i = ep_i^*$ the firm will not be able to price to market (PTM), or, in other words, it will not be able to adjust its markup over costs differently in the two markets in response to an exchange rate change. The ratio of its dollar currency foreign price to its dollar currency home price, $x_i = (ep_i^*)/p_i$, is constrained to remain fixed even when the exchange rate changes. As a result, the elasticity of pricing to market, $\alpha_i = (dx_i/x_i)/(de/e)$, will be zero. *So complete spatial arbitrage always implies zero pricing to market.*

But what about the rate of exchange rate pass-through? As (A2) suggests, this depends on the shape of the firm's cost curve, the elasticity of demand it faces in the two markets, and the relative sizes of the two markets.

CONSTANT OR RISING MARGINAL COSTS. If $c''(Q) \geq 0$ in the neighborhood of $Q$, and the foreign demand curve is less convex than a constant elasticity demand curve (think of the linear demand case), then when the dollar depreciates the foreign demand curve becomes less elastic in dollar terms. As a result, the firm's world (or cumulative) demand curve also becomes less elastic, and the optimal markup over marginal cost (the first term on the right-hand side in equation A2) rises. If the markup rises, and if marginal costs are constant or rising, then the firm's optimal world price in dollars naturally *rises*, say, to $\tilde{p}_I$.

In this situation, pass-through will be incomplete, because, as can be seen by differentiating (A1),

$$(A3) \qquad (dp_i^*/p_i^*) = (dp_i/p_i) - (de/e).$$

That is, the depreciation of the dollar (a rise in $e$), causes foreign currency prices to fall, but the rise in $p_i$ pushes it in the opposite direction. The net result is that foreign currency prices may fall, but they will not fall in full proportion to the exchange rate change (that is, $-1 < (dp_i^*/p_i^*)/(de/e)$). In principle, foreign currency prices might even rise.

FALLING MARGINAL COSTS. If $c''(Q) < 0$, the rate of pass-through depends on the relative slopes of the marginal cost and the new world inverse demand curves. If marginal costs are not falling sufficiently rapidly in relation to the increasing inelasticity of the new world demand—that is, if $|c''(Q)| < |p_i'(Q)|$—then the optimal world price will rise in dollar terms and pass-through will, as before, be incomplete.

But if $|c''(Q)| \geq |p_i'(Q)|$, that is, if marginal costs are falling sufficiently rapidly, then the optimal world price will fall in dollar terms because, even though world demand becomes less elastic and pushes the markup and dollar price higher when the dollar depreciates, the fall in marginal costs pushes prices lower by at least as much. The net effect is that the optimal world price will not rise, and it may even fall if marginal costs are falling sufficiently rapidly. In this case, pass-through will, at a minimum, be complete (that is, $(dp_i^*/p_i^*)/(de/e) \geq 1$).

CONSTANT ELASTICITY. Now return to the case where marginal costs are constant or rising. Let everything else be as before, except assume that the foreign demand curve has constant elasticity. In this case, although the foreign demand elasticity will not change when the dollar depreciates, the share of output sold in the foreign market will rise in response to the dollar's depreciation. This changes the relative shares of the home and foreign markets, which, in turn, could affect the elasticity of world demand and the optimal world price.

Whether it will or not, and in what direction, depends on the relative size of the two demand elasticities. The optimal world dollar price will remain unchanged and pass-through will be complete if both demand elasticities are constant *and* equal, and if marginal costs are constant. If marginal costs are rising, though, the dollar price will rise and pass-through will be incomplete.

If the foreign demand elasticity is equal to or greater than domestic elasticity, that is, $|\bar{\eta}_f| \geq |\eta_{USq}|$, and if marginal costs are constant, then pass-through will, at a minimum, be complete because the new elasticity of world demand will either remain constant (if the two demand elasticities are equal) or rise (since the share of the foreign market has risen), and the optimal world dollar price will either remain the same or fall. However, if marginal costs are rising, then, as the earlier analysis showed, the world price could rise and pass-through could be incomplete. Conversely, if $|\bar{\eta}_f| < |\eta_{USq}|$, then pass-through will be incomplete regardless of whether marginal costs are constant or rising.

OLIGOPOLY. Finally, if the semiconductor device producer was not a monopolist but an oligopolist, then, in the absence of collusion, its initial world price would tend to be closer to its marginal cost. When exchange rates change, the firm will pass through more of the change into foreign currency prices.

This can be seen most easily for the case of constant marginal costs. Write the new world dollar price as $\delta\tilde{p}_i$, where $\tilde{p}_i$ is fixed as the new world dollar price under monopoly, and $1 \leq \delta \leq p_i/\tilde{p}$ for a dollar depreciation, and $p_i/\tilde{p}_i \leq \delta \leq 1$ for a dollar appreciation. The more intense the competition within the oligopoly, the closer will $\delta$ be to $p_i/\tilde{p}_i$, the closer will the new world dollar price be to the old world dollar price, and the more complete will pass-through be. If competition is perfect (see the bottom right-hand corner panel in figure A-1), then $\delta = p_i/\tilde{p}_i$ and the world dollar price remains the same as before (at $p_i$) and pass-through is complete. Conversely, under collusion, $\delta = 1$ and the new world dollar price is $\tilde{p}_I$ (the same as under monopoly).

In summary, the main point is that there is no fixed relationship between arbitrage and the optimal rate of exchange rate pass-through. Incomplete pass-through might be the optimal response in a market with complete spatial arbitrage, whereas complete pass-through might be the optimal response in a market with zero spatial arbitrage (as will be shown in a moment). The actual extent of pass-through will depend on the price elasticities of demand in the home and foreign markets, the relative sizes of the two markets, the slope of the marginal cost curve, and, of course, the degree of competition in the market. Only under fairly narrow conditions (such as sufficiently sharply falling marginal costs, constant and exactly equal demand elasticities at home and abroad, or perfect competition) would complete arbitrage imply complete pass-through.

Therefore, even if American markets were more open than markets in other countries, and even if American producers faced a greater degree of arbitrage pressure compared with firms from Japan or Germany, one needs much more to satisfactorily explain the "more or less complete" pass-through behavior of U.S. exporters implied by the empirical data on U.S. export prices. Besides, in the real world, complete or near complete spatial arbitrage is observed in very few products, whether they are American, German, or Japanese. In subsequent analysis, therefore, it is assumed that markets are separable, and that prices at home and abroad can differ by more than just tariffs and transport costs.

### The Elasticity of Demand

If a price discriminating monopolist faces separable markets and a constant elasticity of demand abroad, then the monopolist's optimal response to an exchange rate change is to completely pass through to foreign prices the effects of the change. A question then emerges: Might constant elasticity demand functions explain the behavior of U.S. export prices?

Consider a U.S. monopolist who produces at home and sells at home and abroad. Arbitrage in the good produced is not possible, and so separate prices can be set in each market. Maximum profits are achieved when markups over common marginal cost are based on the individual demand elasticities in each market.

How should the monopolist change foreign currency prices when the dollar depreciates? From the monopolist's first order condition, the change in foreign currency price is given by:

$$(E1) \qquad dp_i^* = d\lambda^* \cdot \frac{c'(Q)}{e} + \frac{\lambda^*}{e} \cdot c''(Q) + p_i^* \cdot \frac{de}{e},$$

where $\lambda^* = \eta_f / (\eta_f - 1)$ represents the markup abroad (and other variables take the same meanings as before). The interesting result from (E1) is that if marginal costs and the elasticity of foreign demand are constant (that is, $d\eta_f = d\lambda^* = c''(Q) = 0$), then pass-through will be complete and no pricing to market (PTM) will occur. In order for pricing to market to occur in the monopoly case, elasticities and thus markups "must vary with prices."[4]

But it is highly unlikely that U.S. producers across a whole spectrum of manufacturing industries faced foreign demand curves with a particular functional form, namely, constant elasticity. More important, even if they did all face constant elasticity demand curves, once oligopoly is introduced, constant elasticity demand functions do not ensure complete pass-through.

Take the case of a homogeneous good duopoly between a U.S. and a foreign producer. If competition is Bertrand, then equal marginal costs are a precondition for both firms to have positive sales (equal to one-half market-wide sales). Now suppose the dollar depreciates. The American producer gets an asymmetric cost advantage and the foreign firm is forced to exit.[5]

In these circumstances, constant elasticity demand does not ensure complete pass-through. The new foreign price that the American producer will set, and the extent to which it will reflect the cheaper dollar, depends upon the size of the exchange rate change and the shape of the foreign demand curve. As can be seen from figure A-2, if the monopoly foreign price of the U.S. producer,

**Figure A-2.** *Exchange Rate Pass-Through under Monopoly and Constant Elasticity Assumptions*

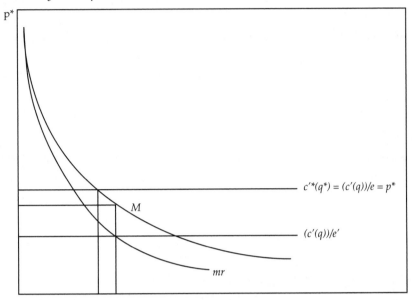

$M$, is less than the marginal cost of the foreign producer, $c'^*(q^*)$, then the new foreign price will be the U.S. producer's monopoly price. Otherwise, the new foreign price that maximizes profit, $c'^*(q^*) - \varepsilon$, is set just below the foreign producer's marginal cost.[6] In neither case will pass-through be complete.[7]

The Cournot (quantity competition) homogeneous goods case provides another useful example.[8] Here price depends not just on the elasticity of demand, but also on the share of market held. In general,

(E2)
$$p_i^* = \left(\frac{\eta_f}{\eta_f - s_f}\right) \cdot \left(\frac{c'(q^*)}{e}\right),$$

where $s_f$ is the share of the foreign market held by the U.S. firm. In general, the larger its share of the foreign market, the higher the

American firm's foreign price. When the dollar depreciates, even if demand abroad is of constant elasticity, prices abroad will not drop to the full extent of the exchange rate change because the U.S. firm gains share in the foreign market. As a result, pass-through will be incomplete.

Whether or not this will lead to PTM depends on how prices at home change. If the two Cournot duopolists have interpenetrated one another's markets, then "pricing behavior in the two markets will be identical, and there will be no pricing to market."[9]

The main point is this: even in the presence of constant elasticity demand functions, categorical statements about pass-through or pricing-to-market behavior cannot be made. But the fact that price-cost margins in imperfectly competitive markets are a function of demand elasticities means that $\eta$ is a critical variable in determining the extent to which pricing to market occurs.

### *The Reaction of Rivals*

The illustrations considered until now either assumed monopoly or homogeneous goods competition among oligopolists. But, in reality, firms produce differentiated products and engage in price competition.[10] In such situations, firms' conjectures about the reaction of rivals become critically important in determining the optimal foreign pricing response to exchange rate changes.

Consider the case of a U.S. producer, firm $i$, whose foreign demand is given by:

(R1) $$q_i^* = q_i^*(p_1^*, p_2^*, \ldots, p_n^*),$$

where $n$ is the total number of firms competing in the market. Since products are heterogeneous, multiple prices can prevail and the quantity demanded depends on own and relative prices. Under profit maximization, firm $i$'s price in foreign currency terms is given by:

$$\text{(R2)} \quad p_i^* = \left[ \frac{\eta_{fi} - \sigma(n-1)\zeta_{ij}}{\eta_{fi} - \sigma(n-1)\zeta_{ij} - 1} \right] \cdot \left[ \frac{c_i'(Q)}{e} \right]; \ \sigma = \sum_{j \neq i} \frac{\partial q_i^*}{\partial p_j^*} \cdot \frac{dp_j^*}{dp_i^*} \bigg/ \sum_{j \neq i} \frac{\partial q_i^*}{\partial p_j^*};$$

where $\eta_{fi}$ is the own price elasticity of firm $i$ when $\partial p_j^*/\partial p_i^* = 0$; $\sigma$ is the firm $i$'s combined conjecture about how all other firms will react to a change in $p_i^*$; and $\zeta_{ji}$ is the cross-price elasticity of $q_i^*$ with respect to $p_j^*$, assuming, for convenience, that prices are initially equal (that is, $p_j^* = p_i^*; j \neq i$).

It can be shown that firm $i$'s price-marginal cost markup in this case is given by:[11]

$$\text{(R3)} \qquad PCM_i^* = \frac{1}{\eta^* + (1-\sigma)(n-1)\zeta_{ji}},$$

where $\eta^*$ is the elasticity of "market" demand abroad (that is, it is producer $i$'s belief about how total quantities abroad will respond when all firms change prices proportionately).

How should firm $i$ change its price-cost margins abroad when the U.S. dollar depreciates? As (R3) suggests, the answer depends critically, among other things, on $\sigma$, firm $i$'s conjecture about how its rivals will respond to a change in $p_i^*$.

COLLUSION CONJECTURE. Consider the case where $\sigma = 1$. If $\sigma = 1$, a price change by firm $i$ is fully matched by other firms. In this case, (R3) collapses to the familiar monopoly case where $PCM_i^* = 1/\eta^*$. As before, what matters now is the shape of the foreign demand curve. As long as foreign demand is less convex than a constant elasticity demand function, the price-cost margin will rise when the dollar depreciates and pass-through will be incomplete. This much is familiar.

BERTRAND CONJECTURE. Consider the case where $\sigma = 0$. If $\sigma = 0$, then (R3) gives the Bertrand result for differentiated products. It is easiest to see this for the duopoly case. Here $n = 2$ and $PCM_i^* = 1/(\eta^* + \zeta_{ji})$. The more substitutable $j$ is for $i$, the higher the cross-price elasticity, and the lower the optimal price-marginal cost markup. When the dollar depreciates, the absolute and relative foreign currency price of *i* drops, and so long as demand is not of constant elasticity, *i*'s price-cost margin will rise. If margins rise when the dollar drops, then, by implication, the exchange rate change was not completely passed through in the form of lower prices. So pass-through will be incomplete once again.

In the extreme case where the products are perfect substitutes, the cross-price elasticity is equal to the market-demand elasticity and price-cost margins collapse to zero. In this case, the situation reverts to the homogeneous goods case.

IN-BETWEEN CONJECTURE. Finally, consider the case where $0 < \sigma < 1$. Here again, when the dollar depreciates and firm *i* drops its foreign price as a result, its relative price drops too, since $\sigma < 1$. This means its price-cost margin in the foreign market will rise and pass-through will, yet again, be incomplete.

Is firm *i* pricing to market in these cases? This depends on whether and how much firm *i* changes prices at home. On the basis of cases considered earlier, it would seem safe to say that even if foreign and home producers had interpenetrated one another's markets, only under quite restrictive assumptions would firm *i* change prices at home in such a manner so as to keep the ratio of prices at home and abroad constant.

### *Importance of Market Share and Expectations about the Permanence of Exchange Rate Changes*

In the previous illustrations, pass-through and pricing-to-market behavior in response to exchange rate changes were analyzed within the context of single-period models. But, in reality, the time horizon relevant for business decisions of this sort is much longer. To paraphrase Raymond Vernon, large enterprises see such decisions as just singular moves in a "campaign stretching across time."[12]

What is the optimal pricing response to exchange rate changes when the dynamics of longer horizons are considered? What role do expectations about the future course of exchange rates play? Do exchange rate changes that are considered temporary elicit smaller responses, as intuition would suggest, than permanent changes?

Perhaps no economic variable plays a more critical role in determining the "answers" to these questions than does market share. In most durable and branded goods industries (which means in most industries in which U.S. firms compete abroad), market share is a critical variable linking the past to the present and the present to the future.

Deeply aware of this fact, large, especially multinational, enterprises jealously guard their hard-won positions in markets across the world, often even when it entails sacrificing some current profits. Inherent in this decision is the belief that market share is an *investment* that will pay sufficiently high dividends in the form of higher future sales and profits.[13] Where this belief is valid, there is a cross-elasticity between present actions and future outcomes, and, naturally, a cross-elasticity between expectations about future events and present actions.

Suppose an American firm plans to sell its goods abroad over two periods.[14] Demand in the first period is given by $q_1^*(p_1^*)$, and by $q_2^*(p_1^*,p_2^*)$ in the second period. Note that first-period prices not only determine first-period sales but also cast a shadow over second-period sales. Demand in the second period is thus written to be a function of lagged prices. Marginal costs are given by $c/e_1$ and $c/e_2$, and the firm maximizes

(M1) $$\left(p_1^* - \frac{c}{e_1}\right) \cdot q_1^*(p_1^*) + \rho\left(p_2^* - \frac{c}{e_2}\right) \cdot q_2^*(p_1^*,p_2^*),$$

where $\rho$ is a discount factor.

How will a temporary change in the exchange rate, say, a depreciation of the dollar (an increase in $e_1$), affect prices?

As seen numerous times above, in the static case (where the exchange rate depreciation is considered permanent), the producer is likely to drop his foreign price, $p_1^*$. This conclusion remains here too. But now there is an additional question: Will an expected fall in $e_2$, a future appreciation of the dollar, lead to a rise in $p_1^*$ and offset, to some extent, the fall in $p_1^*$ caused by the rise in $e_1$?

The answer depends on the relationship between second-period benefits and first-period prices. This is given by

(M2)
$$\Phi = \left(\frac{dX_2^*}{dp_1^*}\right)\left(p_2^* - \frac{c}{e_2}\right) < 0,$$

where $X_2^*$ is quantity sold in the second period. Following Krugman (1987), this can be rewritten in terms of cross-elasticities as

(M3)
$$\Phi = \frac{[(dX_2^*/dp_1^*)(p_1^*/X_2^*)]\left[\left(p_2^* - \frac{c}{e_2}\right)X_2^*\right]}{p_1^*}.$$

From (M3) it can be seen that an anticipated appreciation of the dollar (fall in $e_2$), makes second-period sales less valuable (that is, $\partial\Phi/\partial e_2 > 0$). Therefore, it becomes less worthwhile to trade off first-period profits by lowering first-period prices in order to capture higher second-period sales. As a result, the expected appreciation will lead the producer to raise first-period prices as long as the cross-elasticity between first-period prices and second-period sales does not change when $e_2$ falls.

In terms of optimal responses to exchange rate changes, this suggests that exchange rate changes believed to be temporary are less likely to elicit as sizable a response as those believed to be permanent. Of course, whether or not the producer will ultimately raise or lower first-period prices depends on the relative magnitudes of the additional first-period profits captured by raising prices and the forgone second-period profits lost as a result of the same action: "Here as elsewhere . . . , the answer seems to be contingent on functional form."[15]

THE DISCOUNT FACTOR. Beyond the functional form of the demand curves, as Kenneth Froot and Paul Klemperer show in their two-period duopoly model, the answer must also depend on whether the producer's discount factor, $\rho$, changes when the exchange rate changes.[16] Froot and Klemperer relate the discount factor to exchange rates by the uncovered interest parity condition:

(M4) $\qquad \rho = \rho^F = \rho^{US} e_1/e_2; \qquad \rho^i = 1/(1 + r^i);$

where the $r^i$s are the interest rates in the United States and abroad.[17] (This condition ensures that riskless arbitrage is not possible on the forward exchange market.) Assuming, for simplicity, that interest rates in the U.S. remain constant when $e_1$ changes (or when $e_2$ is expected to change), the interest rate abroad and the discount factor, $\rho$, must change for (M4) to hold.[18]

How might the American producer change foreign prices in response to a temporary depreciation of the dollar (that is, to $de_1 > 0$)? Unlike before, the answer now has two components to it. The first component, as before, relates to how the American producer's costs change in foreign currency terms, and the second, and new component, relates to how the discount factor moves.

The whole effect of incorporating M4 into the analysis can be seen in the producer's first-order condition, which stipulates:

(M5) $\qquad \left| \dfrac{\partial \pi_1^*}{\partial p_1^*} \right| = \left| \rho \left( \dfrac{\partial \pi_2^*}{\partial \theta^*} \right) \left( \dfrac{\partial \theta^*}{\partial p_1^*} \right) \right|,$

where $\pi_t^*$ is the firm's foreign currency profit in period $t$; and $\theta^*$ is the firm's first-period foreign market share (which is a function of the firm's first-period foreign currency relative price). Equation (M5) balances "the marginal cost of further market-share investment through lower prices [in period one] . . . against the marginal return from this investment," which is received in period two.[19]

When a temporary depreciation occurs, $c/e_1$, the American firm's marginal cost measured in foreign currency falls. This encourages the American firm to lower its foreign currency price. This is the first and familiar component of the answer.

The second and new component relates to the discount factor in (M4). When a temporary depreciation occurs, $e_1$ rises and $\rho$, the discount factor, rises to maintain uncovered interest parity. (Note, as written here, when the discount *factor* rises, the discount *rate* drops.) When $\rho$ rises, the right-hand side of (M5) becomes larger and the equality condition is violated. In order to return to equality, the left-hand side of (M5) must rise. This, in turn, implies that the American firm must raise its period-one prices.

The intuition behind this result is that when the dollar depreciates temporarily, each unit of foreign currency earned in period one becomes more valuable in dollar terms in relation to those to be earned in period two. As a result, the relative value of period-two sales decreases. This reduces the firm's incentive to invest in market share through lower period-one prices. Hence the motivation to raise price.

The net result of a temporary dollar depreciation is thus ambiguous if the discount factor changes when the exchange rate changes. The "cost effects" encourage the producer to lower first-period foreign currency prices, while the "interest rate effects" encourage the producer to raise first-period foreign currency prices. In theory, it is possible for the latter effect to dominate and for the American producer to raise foreign currency prices in the face of a temporary dollar depreciation.

In reality, though, "expected future exchange rates move strongly with current rates: exchange rate changes are predominantly permanent."[20] This makes perverse pass-through very unlikely to occur, because in the case of a permanent exchange rate change, $de_1 = de_2$, and the discount factor, $\rho$, remains unchanged. As a result, there is no interest rate effect. The only effect remaining is the cost effect, which accords with intuition and predicts that when the dollar depreciates, the American firm will lower its foreign currency price.

EXPECTED DEPRECIATION. Finally, in the case of an expected future depreciation of the dollar (where $de_1 = 0$; $de_2 > 0$), both the cost effect and the interest rate effect operate in the same direction and encourage the producer to drop first-period prices and invest in more market share. The interest rate effect is equal in magnitude but opposite in sign to a temporary exchange rate effect.

This means that an expected future exchange rate change *may* have a larger impact on current prices than a current and permanent exchange rate change. Since the second-period cost effects cancel out in both cases, this will happen only when the interest rate effects of the expected exchange rate change dominate the first-period cost effects of the permanent exchange rate change. The interest rate effect will dominate "if a sufficiently small fraction of costs are fixed" in the firm's home currency.[21]

In reality, as chapter 3 showed, America's largest exporters, its MNEs, commonly incur large portions of their costs outside the United States. This fact, coupled with Froot and Klemperer's model, leads to a hierarchy of predicted effects of exchange rate changes on American MNEs' foreign currency prices:

(M6)    $dp^*_{\text{TEMPORARY CHG}} < dp^*_{\text{PERMANENT CHG}} < dp^*_{\text{EXPECTED CHG}}$.

American firms are likely to change foreign currency prices least (or perhaps not at all) in response to a temporary exchange rate change; by more in response to a permanent exchange rate change; and by the most in response to an expected permanent exchange rate change. Furthermore, "Greater uncertainty about future exchange rates may . . . [increase] the expected value of . . . market share to a risk-neutral . . . firm" and may strengthen the movement of current prices.[22]

What does the market share story suggest for pass-through and pricing to market? The minute the words "market share" and "future matters" are invoked, it becomes intuitively obvious why *temporary* changes in the exchange rate, particularly appreciations of the dollar, are unlikely to be fully passed through to foreign currency prices. It might even be intuitive that temporary depreciations might not be fully passed through; each unit of foreign currency earned today is suddenly, but only temporarily, more valuable than those that will be earned tomorrow.

But if market share matters, will a U.S. firm not be better off by fully lowering its foreign currency price in the face of a "permanent" drop in the value of the dollar? That is, would pass-through not be complete? The answer is, not necessarily. In imperfectly competitive markets where search and switching costs, brand loyalty, network externalities, and so on, matter, an increase in market share makes future demand less elastic. But for these same reasons, current demand also becomes less elastic: "While first-period competition is increased by each firm's expectation that market share will help it in the future, the consumers' realization that firms with higher market shares will charge higher prices in the future makes demand less elastic and thus reduces first-period competition."[23] This, in turn, makes it optimal for firms to take higher current markups even in the face of permanent dollar depreciation.

In summary, the levels of and changes in markups ultimately depend upon the nature of demand (and the shape of the demand curve), the structure of markets (and the nature of competition), and, perhaps most important, on the reactions (and conjectures about reactions) of rival players in the context of repeated games. Permanent exchange rate changes simply create (or add to existing) asymmetries between rivals. The portion of such changes that finally gets passed through to prices depends on these fundamental factors, and not on whether the changes are appreciations or depreciations. Hence market share and dynamics-related hypotheses are also unlikely to explain any empirical findings of complete pass-through in the behavior of U.S. export prices.

# Case Studies of Responses to the Dollar at Three U.S. Firms | B

CHAPTERS 2 AND 3 of this book have shown that when the appropriate data are examined, American firms, as theory would predict, appear to price and source strategically in response to exchange rate changes. Nevertheless, since these findings, especially on pricing, run counter to widely held views on these issues, it is useful to go beyond modeling and empirical analyses and explore their validity at the level of the firm.

In this spirit, we interviewed senior executives at three large U.S. firms (two of which are among America's top exporters) on the subject of exchange rate changes and U.S. firm responses. The officers were asked a series of general and specific questions about whether and how their firms responded in their foreign market pricing and sourcing strategies to the sharp fall in the dollar during the latter half of the 1980s.

They were asked about the pricing *process* within their firms, the role of transfer prices, the factors influencing their external pricing decisions, movements in their profit margins, and such. Where possible, specific illustrations were solicited. Finally, the officers were asked to comment on the competing hypotheses advanced by this and prior research in light of their cumulative experience in dealing with exchange rate changes and their knowledge of normal business practice.

As the interview excerpts demonstrate, none of the officers indicated that the notions surmised from the analyses in this book were wrong or misplaced. Whereas they said that these hypotheses were "pretty right," they viewed much less favorably the competing hypotheses, especially in the pricing area. In fact, when confronted with the view that American firms tend to allow their foreign market prices to vary one for one with the dollar, one officer responded, "I know of no company that does this!"

The interviewees also provided some fascinating illustrations that highlighted the limited role of arbitrage, the fallacy of the "export sales are marginal" argument proposed in prior research, and some important limitations of the U.S. export price data. One illustration clearly demonstrated that pricing-to-market behavior by U.S. firms was not limited to the dollar *depreciation* phase; it also applied during *appreciations* (when U.S. firms had to shrink their foreign profit margins as they attempted to stabilize foreign currency prices and maintain customers).

These findings, which reinforce both the central and the adjunct hypotheses proffered by this study, appear remarkably similar to the findings of David Sharp in his 1987 study of multinational firms, for which he interviewed ten firms on related issues during the 1984–85 high-dollar period.[1] Since they are so closely related to the issues at hand, Sharp's more detailed findings will be cited from time to time in this chapter.

Before proceeding, some clarifications must be made. First, because the interviews were of limited duration (lasting no more than two hours each), a trade-off had to be made between the *breadth* of the issues covered and the *depth* in which they could be discussed. The trade-off was made in favor of depth, and emphasis was placed on exploring the pricing issue more closely, because it seemed more puzzling and less amenable to empirical analysis than the sourcing issue. Consequently, although it was broached during every interview, sourcing receives only passing mention in this chapter.

Second, the behavior of three firms (though very large) cannot provide a sound basis on which to *substantiate* the pricing and sourcing hypotheses favored by this study. That task is left to chapters 2 and 3. Instead, the limited aim here is to determine whether the views surmised from the data at higher levels of aggregation hold up when the unit of analysis is the firm (or a decisionmaking unit such as a division within a firm). If these hypotheses hold even at this level, then validity and robustness will have been enhanced.

The next section introduces the firms and describes their relevant characteristics. Interview findings follow.

## The Firms and How They Were Selected

Corporate managers are extremely hesitant to discuss matters as sensitive as their firm's pricing strategies with outsiders (especially if they suspect—albeit wrongly in this case—that the questioner is interested in the firm's international transfer pricing policies and its *tax* implications).

By necessity, therefore, the interviews were obtained through a network of (indirect) personal contacts with senior officers.[2] Admittedly, this meant that the firms were not selected on a set of preestablished objective criteria; rather, the firms selected themselves. The only requirement imposed was that the firms be involved in exporting manufactured goods from the United States and that they compete actively in foreign markets.

In this manner, three *Fortune 500* firms—call them firm A, firm B, and firm C—were identified. At firm A, two separate sets of interviews were conducted at two distinct divisions that participated in quite different businesses. Combined annual sales at the three firms come close to $80 billion, although one firm is very large, one is of moderate size, and one is *relatively* small. All three sell durable, large-ticket, commercial products, but two also sell nondurable, small-ticket, consumer products. Typical of America's key exporters, all three are multinational enterprises, and all three are in oligopolistic, high-technology industries (telecommunications equipment, machinery, and optical equipment and supplies). Certain other relevant information about these firms is presented in table B-1. The information is disguised and kept superficial in order to conceal the identity of the firms.

As table B-1 shows, beyond the similarities observed above, several characteristics set the firms apart. The three firms are in quite different industries, possess different networks of production capabilities, and have varying levels of market power in their international markets (not shown). How the firms deployed these varying capabilities to deal with exchange rate changes is the focus of the next section. It is not obvious from this information how, in fact, these firms would respond to changing exchange rates.

At one of the firms, exports account for a small share of overall sales. For one firm, the threat of arbitrage is very high, since the weight-to-value ratio of its main product is relatively low, and the firms' products require no specialized installation or after-sales service.

When related to the hypotheses advanced by prior research, these characteristics would suggest that these firms are unlikely to price to market when the exchange rate changes. In fact, the U.S. dollar export price index for the four-digit SIC that one of these firms dominates shows almost no change between 1985 and 1989 even as the dollar tumbled in this firm's main foreign markets.

**Table B-1. Selected Details on the Firms Studied**

| Firm | Representative products | Product and industry characteristics | Nationality of key competitors | Scale of overseas production in product areas examined | Foreign sales as a percentage of total sales | Exports as a percentage of total sales |
|---|---|---|---|---|---|---|
| Firm A, Division 1 | Telecommunications equipment | Moderately differentiated; oligopoly; moderate entry barriers | American, Japanese, French | No overseas manufacturing; but when desirable, some inputs sourced from abroad | ≈ 85 | ≈ 85 |
| Firm A, Division 2 | Instrumentation | Not differentiated; oligopoly; low entry barriers | American, Japanese, Israeli | Some overseas customizing | n.a. | n.a. |
| Firm B | Machinery | Differentiated; oligopoly; high entry barriers | Japanese, German | Significant overseas manufacturing operations; foreign plants are product focused | ≈ 30 | ≈ 20 |
| Firm C | Optical equipment and supplies | Moderately differentiated; oligopoly; high entry barriers | American, Japanese | Significant overseas manufacturing operations; foreign plants are production function focused | ≈ 50 | ≈ 15 |

Source: Authors' fieldwork; firm public reports.
n.a. Not available.

On the other hand, two of the firms advertise extensively (thereby undertaking classic sunk costs) in the foreign markets they participate in; two invest heavily in developing their markets and face long sales cycles; two are in industries where current market shares and long-term customer relationships matter a great deal (and where price is only one of several factors influencing the purchasing decision); and all are in oligopolistic markets with foreign rivals operating from quite different production and cost structures. When related to the theory on pricing to market, these characteristics would lead one to believe that these firms do price to market abroad. Hence, although not randomly selected, the three firms considered here seem well suited to our purposes. How, in fact, did these firms behave and what insights do they offer? These questions are addressed next.

## The Pricing Process

At two of the three firms, foreign market pricing was clearly a two-stage process. In the first stage, exports were made to foreign affiliates at intrafirm transfer prices, and in the second stage, these affiliates sold the products at prices they decided locally (often in conjunction with the U.S. parents). Intrafirm transfer prices were based on costs and were universally thought of as being only one among several factors influencing the external prices charged arm's-length foreign customers.

Here is how the executive at the machinery company explained it:

> We centralize our forex risk management in the headquarters because we believe we have the scale and the expertise to manage this risk here. . . .
>
> But there is definitely a two-stage pricing process. Our subsidiaries make their sales primarily to their local markets. They make

these sales in their local currencies and they have the autonomy to decide how they want to compete.

The interviewee at the optical products company indicated that foreign pricing at his firm was also done in a two-stage process because the firm owned its distribution network worldwide and made almost all its exports intrafirm. He explained how transfer prices were established at his firm:

> Intrafirm transfer prices are set in dollars. . . . The worldwide business manager is responsible for establishing this price. Manufacturing at [our firm] is a cost center not a profit center. So typically the transfer price is a cost or cost-plus price. But since tax agencies in foreign countries are becoming very active in this area, [the firm] is moving more and more toward straight cost billing.
>
> External prices depend on several factors, key among which are cost, competition and our country strategy. . . . But none of these external prices involves a one-for-one change with the exchange rate.

Even at division 1 of the telecommunications equipment company, where intrafirm shipments were rare, when they took place, the process was similar:

> Firstly, we don't really transship a lot. Our most important and largest sales are made by us from here in [the U.S.].
>
> When we do transship, there are two ways of pricing the sub. If the order is small, say, $50K to $100K, then we just charge them the list price minus, say, a 15 percent discount. The list price is published once a year. Of course, this list price need bear no resemblance to the price they turn around and charge their customer. That external price is dependent on the market.
>
> In the second instance, if the order is actually large, which it rarely is, then the sub can directly contract with the manufacturing facility and get a cost-plus price.

At division 2 of the telecommunications equipment company, the manager noted that about 35 percent of the firm's foreign sales were made through its subsidiaries. Here, too, intrafirm prices were cost-based, but external prices were market driven:

> Let's talk about our pricing to the subs. What we have is a catalog list price that we quote them. This price is a cost plus margin price. Now when the dollar was high, as in 1985, the subs would request discounts from us on these list prices and we'd give it to them. But when things are going well, because the dollar is low, then we don't hear from them, but they still pay us the same catalog price.
>
> Now the key thing is that their external price is not affected one for one by the dollar's drop. In fact, they may be selling at twice the dollar price in Europe as we are here. . . .
>
> In short, the external price is really a market price and that's what we will meet. Our internal prices just reflect a cost plus pricing.
>
> But there is no question that we have different margins in different parts of the world for the same product and at the same time. We price to market.

The managers were also asked to describe how their external prices were decided: "Where and how do you decide your foreign market price? What role do exchange rates play?"

At division 1 of the telecommunications equipment company, as noted earlier, production was entirely U.S.-based and foreign sales were typically made through exports. In this respect, among the three firms interviewed this firm was the most exposed to changes in the dollar's exchange rate. But as the division president's response indicates, at his firm, too, it was the market situation, not the exchange rate, that drove foreign market prices:

> Note, rarely is price the most important competitive variable. Performance and reputation are much more important.
>
> We base our pricing on what the market will bear. We have an "extremely flexible" pricing policy. There is no difference between us and [our Japanese competitor].
>
> Our pricing essentially starts with a detailed bottom-up construction of all the costs involved in executing the project. We also construct a cost estimate for our key competitors based on our understanding of their costs and past experience of how they bid. Finally,

we also gather detailed information on the [customer's] budget for this project. Based on these, the sales manager in charge will make a proposal to the senior management on what [we] should bid. He is then interrogated on each and every element of this cost construction and the other relevant facts. These facts may include things like whether the [customer] favors the Japanese or the French and whatever other nonprice facts there may be.

The key thing is that there is perfect information between us and our competitors on most matters concerning a job. So we are extremely sensitive to market conditions.

Finally, there are human factors here. I am involved in a battle with my counterpart at [the Japanese firm], Mr. [X]. I know every move that he is likely to make and similarly, he does my moves. We each want to win this thing and there is a very personal rivalry here which economists never understand or model. I want to be able to see him at the next conference or what-have-you and say, "That last one was a tough one, wasn't it?"

At the optical products company, price leadership was noted to be critical. The firm had a preeminent brand name and dominant market share worldwide, and as a result what mattered to it was the integrity of the signal that its price differential sent:

The most important factor in [our external] pricing is the competition's price. [Our Japanese competitors'] price is about 10 to 15 percent below us, and [our European] competitors a bit below that. Finally, the private label makers price 35 to 40 percent below us. We want to maintain this standard price leader differential with them.

There are two other reasons why we won't cut our foreign market prices to get a march on our competition. One, we miss the opportunity to get a better price—and thus high margins—and two, we face grey market pressure if we go too much out of line. . . .

The whole issue is market power. If you are in a position like ours, with power over dealers and such, then you can manage your pricing. If you are in a highly competitive situation like some of our [other] divisions might be, then you are a price taker. . . .

But I know of no company that would change its foreign market prices one for one with the exchange rate! At least no [large] company. We are in it for the long run. If we change our prices wildly, then we will be seen as opportunists. If we do this, we will not be able to get the consumption patterns we are trying to promote in the target market. We spend a ton of money on advertising and promotion and by bringing unstable prices into the line of vision of our customers we will frustrate these marketing efforts. . . .

[So] external prices depend on several factors . . . but none of these external prices involves a one-for-one change with the exchange rate.

The sentiments expressed by the officer at the machinery company were quite similar:

The bottom line is we want to be competitive in our markets, but we won't lower our prices any more than we have to. . . .

The key question is who is this customer and how important are they to us? If the relationship is long-term, then we will shrink our margins and accommodate this customer because we want to remain a big player in the market in the future and we know that exchange rates might change again.

Again, typically there are those 20 percent of our customers who generate 80 percent of our sales and profits. For these customers, we are not going to completely pass through to their local currency prices the higher dollar.

It seems clear from these excerpts that competitive factors held a high place in the consciousness of these managers, but that exchange rates did not feature nearly as prominently. Where the subject came up in the interviews, respondents clearly stated that exchange rate *changes* do not play a major role in influencing external pricing decisions.

These managers accorded such low importance to exchange rate changes for a variety of reasons: price was rarely *the* determining variable in the purchaser's decision (implying that products were differentiated and competition was oligopolistic); prices were also used as signals and hence not suited to much fluctuation (without the loss of reputation);[3] arbitrage and market power (particularly over distributors) played a role; firms had a long decisionmaking horizon when it came to deciding today's prices and were willing to forgo opportunistic moves in the interest of future competitiveness and market position; customer *relationships* mattered for the same reason; and "winning" in personal business rivalries mattered.

Although prior research has reached the opposite conclusion regarding the role of exchange rate changes in the foreign market pricing policies of U.S. firms, it is to their credit that many of the factors listed above resonate in the theoretical models developed to explain the pricing-to-market behavior of Japanese and German firms in the United States.

To get a better sense of how these firms respond to exchange rate *changes* in their foreign market pricing, we took the interviewees through some simple exchange rate change scenarios and also asked them to give their own illustrations.

## Pricing When the Exchange Rate Changes

When asked how his firm's foreign market prices would move if the dollar depreciated, as it did during the latter half of the 1980s, the machinery company executive responded:

> We will use this as an opportunity to either become the market share leader and/or boost our margins.
>
> Let's take the [hospital] equipment business where we compete against [a German firm] and [a Japanese firm]. Let's say we were involved in a sale in Japan. If the dollar drops sharply—say, as it did during the post-1985 period—and if we know that [the German firm] is fully hedged in the DM/¥ market, then we know that every time they cut their yen price, they are cutting into their margins. Similarly, we know that unless [the Japanese firm] can outsource its components from the United States or cut its costs sharply, it will also be taking shrinking margins to compete against us. So in this situation,

we will cut our yen prices very little or by as much as we have to get the sale and the higher market share, and we will take higher margins.

The bottom line is we want to be competitive in our markets, but we won't lower our prices any more than we have to.

Asked whether his firm would find foreign currency price stabilization an attractive strategy even when the dollar *appreciated*, the officer responded with this fascinating illustration:

Right now we are engaged in a deal with [an appliance manufacturer] in Sweden where we are supplying to them [a key component] that they fit in their [products]. Now the dollar has been rising sharply against the Swedish krone and we sell these units to them in dollars. Obviously, [the Swedish firm] is quite worried about this situation.

Presently we sell about $3 million worth to them, but the business manager [whose division supplies this unit] feels that this business is going to grow to about $25 million in the next two to three years. Therefore, this is an important customer for us. So we have entered into an alliance with the Swedish firm to handle the exchange rate risk issue. If the exchange rate moves within a 5 percent band of our agreed-upon base rate, then each firm bears that risk by itself. But for every movement beyond the 5 percent band, we split the risk evenly. That is, we share the currency risk with them.

So similarly, we have other important customers and we are not going to lose their business because exchange rates fluctuate. Of course, this is not going to be the case with our less important customers.

To begin with, this illustration provides casual evidence to support a view that is consistent with theory, namely, that American firms, like their Japanese and German counterparts in the United States, are willing to shrink their foreign profit margins in order to maintain share when the currency moves unfavorably. This suggests that the central finding of chapter 2—that American firms priced to market during the dollar-depreciation period of the latter half of the 1980s—is also likely to hold for the dollar-appreciation period of the early half of the 1980s.

But the illustration raises an even more interesting point. When one remembers that the annual sales of this firm run in the billions of dollars, why would such a gigantic firm treat a $3 million Swedish customer as "important" rather than "marginal." It appears that the importance of a customer (and the degree to which a sale is considered "marginal") is not decided at the broadest corporate level, but at the level of the business unit. To a division manager in charge of $200 million dollars or so of revenue, the prospect of developing a $25 million customer could seem enormously attractive and easily justify incurring special "menu costs" and taking tighter margins in the short run.

This throws serious doubt on the hypothesis that "American firms do not price to market because their export sales are marginal." Company-wide sales—the denominator normally used in these calculations—can be an inappropriate and misleading yardstick by which to gauge the importance of a firm's exports. This is especially true for American exporters, because they *tend* to be very large enterprises that participate in multiple businesses and are divisionalized either by product or geography. And unless the (present) value of firm exports is assessed in relation to the appropriate and smaller decisionmaking units whose bottom lines these exports affect, predictions about export-pricing behavior assuming a corporate level perspective stand a good chance of being wrong.

In an attempt to corroborate the interviewee's assertions that his company flexes its margins in order to counter movements in the exchange rate, we examined profit margins for the most export-oriented division (around whose products the interview centered) for the decade of the 1980s. The available data are shown in table B-2 (in a normalized form to conceal the identity of the firm). Since the firm restructured its divisions in 1982, two sets of calculations

**Table B-2.** *Operating Margins at the Most Export-Oriented Division of the Machinery Firm, 1980–90*[a]

| Year | Classification | |
|------|------|------|
|      | *1* | *2* |
| 1980 | 100 | ... |
| 1981 | 87 | ... |
| 1982 | 75 | 100 |
| 1983 | ... | 79 |
| 1984 | ... | 0 |
| 1985 | ... | 9 |
| 1986 | ... | 38 |
| 1987 | ... | 77 |
| 1988 | ... | 111 |
| 1989 | ... | 133 |
| 1990 | ... | 127 |

Source: Firm public reports, 1980–90.

a. Operating margin equals (sales – cost of goods sold – selling, and general and administrative expenses – depreciation) divided by sales. When depreciation is added back to get one step closer to price-cost margins, the pattern does not change.

are made: one going from 1980 to 1982, and the other from 1982 to 1990.

As figure B-1 shows, the division's operating margins declined sharply during the first half of the 1980s, which saw the dollar appreciate substantially, and then rose sharply after 1985, when the dollar depreciated substantially. To be sure, these data are quite removed from the kind one needs to make definitive statements about pricing-to-market behavior, but they do not appear inconsistent with the pricing behavior described by the interviewee.

### At the Telecommunications Equipment Company

When asked how the telecommunications equipment company would respond in its pricing if the dollar depreciated, its representative offered much the same answer. The president at division 1

**Figure B-1.** *Operating Margins at the Most Export-Oriented Division of the Machinery Firm, 1980–90*

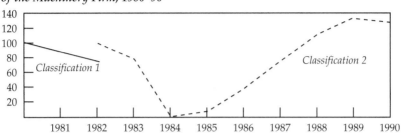

of the firm said that he would use the depreciated exchange rate to reduce his foreign currency price as much as he *had* to, but certainly not by as much as he *could*. (He cannot be quoted verbatim here because his comments on this particular question could not be recorded.)

The president said that his competitors would try to match his downward price moves within a certain price zone, but that after a certain point, they would have to stop. He pointed out that, in the first instance, the competitors would try to get its country's ambassador (in the third country) involved in the effort since his company's products were often procured at the governmental level. If that did not work, his foreign competitors would lower the financing costs for their products, he noted, adding, "Their exim bank works much better than ours." And if that did not work, he continued, then his competitors would shrink their margins on the main product but make up the loss on spares and replacements.

The officer at the telecommunications equipment firm also noted that "time was not zero" between exchange rate changes, and that those affected unfavorably by the exchange rate change would have a chance to adjust their costs down by switching sourcing or improving productivity.

*At the Optical Products Company*

The story was the same at the optical products company. At this firm, the interview revolved around one of the firm's products that sold for about ¥7,500 in Japan.[4] The interviewee was asked how his firm would respond if the dollar dropped by 40 percent in real terms against the yen. Since the firm did no manufacturing in Japan, it would ostensibly need only ¥4,500 to recover the original dollar price of this product:

> We will never drop the yen price to ¥4,500 even though the country manager in Japan may suggest we make this draconian move to beat [our Japanese competitor]. But we probably can't stay at ¥7,500, either. We probably will go to ¥6,000. Again the key reason for going down is that our dealers and retailers know that we are making a ton of money now and they want a piece of the action as well. Otherwise their incentive to arbitrage becomes too high. The way in which we justify keeping the extra ¥1,500 that we do (over the ¥4,500) is by telling the retailers that we will invest these windfall profits in their market in advertising, manufacturing, and such. Basically, they know that we will invest in growing their market.
>
> Furthermore, they know that we get hit on the other side when the dollar goes up. [For instance] we buy our [raw materials] in the United States. So when our raw material prices go up, we have to raise our prices some, but we also eat our margins. So they are sympathetic to our situation.

Clearly, there is no support in these statements for a complete pass-through hypothesis on foreign pricing. Shreds of evidence constructed from this firm's 10-K and annual reports are not inconsistent with the behavior described by the interviewee. One company statement noted that although revenues in the firm's key foreign business had risen by some 30 percent (since the dollar's depreciation), profit *margins* had risen by nearly 400 percent. As figure B-2 shows, movements in this firm's foreign profit margins during the 1980s are not inconsistent with a pricing-to-market story.[5]

**Figure B-2.** *Index of Foreign Operating Income as a Percentage of Foreign Sales at the Optical Products Firm, 1980–90*

Index

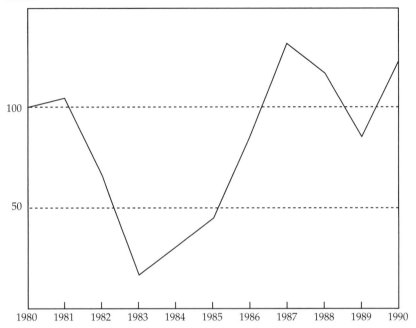

Source: Company reports.

*Sharp's Findings*

In his 1984–85 interviews with business managers at several American firms, David Sharp also repeatedly confronts the view that local currency price stabilization is paramount:

> An assumption held so widely among interviewees that it merits consideration was that the currency of denomination of revenues of a product line was also the currency of its determination; that is, the price would tend to remain constant in that currency. While this is true within the period during which price lists remain unchanged, there is no reason in principle why a price change in any currency

should not fully reflect the intervening movement of the exchange rate with any other currency. A possible explanation is that the currency of invoicing truly is very stable, either as a result of the market economics, or because firms with market power choose to invoice in and stabilise prices in that currency.[6]

Sharp, who conducted his interviews before the pricing-to-market literature was developed, appears to chance upon the answer when he asks the controller at the U.K. manufacturing subsidiary of an American industrial equipment company, "But doesn't the strong dollar make the division uncompetitive?"

Sharp's interviewee responds: "Much of that dollar invoicing I have to say is intercompany, so therefore not a major factor. But there is also a lot of dollar invoicing in the Middle East, where we have become uncompetitive, and we have cut our dollar pricing."[7]

Sharp follows up with the question, "Do prices tend to rise and fall with the dollar?" The controller responds:

> When we have a pricing meeting, the first thing we do is look at the movement of the currencies, then what our competition has done, as far as we guess it, in the invoice currency we know they apply to that market. Then we will attempt to be competitive with them on both those counts. In other words, the landed cost to our dealer in France is going to have to be competitive to the landed cost of [the Japanese competitor]. To that extent, we are offsetting usually; when the currency has gone detrimental, we'll hold the price increase to reflect that, or if it goes up, we can take a bigger price increase, and we do that, but the basic parameter is that the product has to be landed competitively in the market.[8]

Another of Sharp's interviewees notes:

> There are certain fixed discounts depending on exchange fluctuations, because our prices are still all stated in terms of U.S. dollars. So they are automatically adjusted for exchange differences. . . . When the dealer quotes in lire, there can be an adjustment so that he can maintain his lire price. . . . Suppose it was 10,000 lire for the machine,

or $1000, and the dollar strengthens 20%. So now it is 12,000 lire. Then what we are trying to do is to adjust that lire price down as close to 10,000 as possible. We participate with the dealer and give him some financing. . . .

The published prices are fixed in dollars, throughout Europe. Through the exchange stabilization process, we provide a discount to the dealer.[9]

Summarizing his interview findings, Sharp writes, "Price discrimination is the rule rather than the exception, and was the stated objective of all but one [of ten] compan[ies] interviewed."[10] Although the interviews for the present study were conducted several years later (in 1992–93) and at a time when the dollar had strongly depreciated from its highs in 1985, Sharp's surmise still applies.

But, as seen in chapter 2, the U.S. dollar export price index is clearly at odds with these interview findings. Although the interviews indicate that American firms attempt to have stable foreign currency prices in their foreign markets even as the exchange rate changes, the export price index for the latter half of the 1980s suggests precisely the opposite (that is, American firms had stable dollar prices and sharply falling foreign currency prices). The export price index came up at two of the firms interviewed for this study, and both instances highlighted important limitations of the index.

## Limitations of the U.S. Bureau of Labor Statistics Export Price Index

The first instance goes back to a response given earlier at one of the firms interviewed for this study. The interviewee at this firm stated unequivocally that far from passing through exchange rate changes one for one to foreign market prices, his firm attempts to stabilize its foreign currency prices when the exchange rate changes.

Oddly enough, the U.S. dollar export price index published by the Bureau of Labor Statistics (BLS) for the particular *four-digit* SIC that this firm belongs to (and dominates by virtue of its size and export volume) shows virtually no movement during the long and sharp dollar depreciation phase of the mid- to late 1980s. The remarkable constancy of the U.S. dollar export price index for this industry implies that U.S. firms completely passed through changes in the dollar's exchange rates to their foreign customers. As noted earlier, it is on the basis of similar patterns (across a spectrum of manufacturing industries) that prior research has concluded that American firms do not price to market.

How can it be that a firm shows up (as much as "firms" show up) in the BLS dollar export price index as not pricing to market, even though the firm strongly maintains that it does? As we have shown (in chapter 2), the degree of constancy an industry exhibits in its U.S. dollar export price index is highly correlated with the intensity of intrafirm trade in that industry. Hence we speculated that rather than reflecting the arm's-length foreign market price of U.S. products, the export price index in these industries reflects the internal transfer prices that U.S. exporters charge their foreign affiliates.

This logic *seems* to apply well in the case at hand. The annual report of the firm at issue indicates that it transfers the vast majority of its exports to its own affiliates abroad. The interviewee confirmed this and noted further that its exports were typically made on the basis of a set of intrafirm cost-based transfer prices. This explains why, even though the firm had stable local currency prices in its foreign markets (and, by implication, rising dollar export prices during the dollar depreciation phase), the firm's official dollar export price appeared stable. In other words, the two-stage pricing process has the potential to create a *disconnect* between U.S. export prices and market prices charged arm's-length foreign customers, and this appears to be the proximate cause of the paradox. Although this could be an isolated incident, the strong and unexpected correlation observed between export prices and the intensity of intrafirm trade (in chapter 2) suggests that this is unlikely.

This illustration demonstrates one limitation of the BLS export price index. Another limitation was highlighted by the experience of an interviewee at the telecommunications equipment firm. This interviewee had been recently approached by the BLS with a request to participate in the U.S. export price index survey. To get things going, as is the bureau's usual practice, two economists from the BLS had come to visit the firm and select the products whose export prices they would track on a monthly basis through a questionnaire. While the BLS economists were understandably eager to select a couple of long-lived, standardized products for price comparison purposes, they were told that on both accounts this firm would probably not be able to provide meaningful input. The firm's products were not standardized in the usual sense of the word, and its prices varied from customer to customer (and country to country). Nonetheless, at the insistence of the bureau's economists, a compromise was achieved. The officer who dealt with the BLS visitors described it thus:

> I told the economists from the BLS that [our company] sold more systems than products and . . . we priced the same system differently in each country and . . . there really was no such thing as a typical system, let alone product. But the BLS didn't really want to hear about the complexity of the business, they wanted some prices that were "representative."
>
> So I picked three components (of systems that we sell) from the price book and told the BLS that they could perhaps use these, since there would be one price, and that these components would perhaps have a life of about ten years. The published list price of the three products was between $2,000 and $25,000. The list price is calculated on a cost plus margin basis and this price is revised about once or twice a year.

Of course, in actuality, the systems that [we sell] run in the millions of dollars and the price of these components may have no real influence on the final price we charge our customers. Besides, they may be sold at different prices depending on the market and the time.

But since the BLS wanted us to report a price each month, we said we would give them the same price until a new catalog was published even if in the meantime, the actual "price" of these components had changed.

The interviewee's point was that although the BLS wished to collect *transaction* prices, its desire could not be accommodated by his firm because it was unlikely that an exact system sold in any given month, quarter, or year would be transacted again. On the other hand, sampling the internal "catalog" price of a few components would satisfy the comparability criterion but run a high risk of making the index unrepresentative of true market prices. These factors notwithstanding, the firm is now officially part of the BLS export price survey on telecommunications equipment and contributes to the calculation of the index.

To summarize, if export-oriented firms such as the telecommunications company report infrequently changing, cost-based, catalog prices in the BLS export price survey, and if foreign production- and sales-oriented firms such as the one whose exports were primarily intrafirm report cost-based transfer prices, then one should not be surprised to find a disconnect between the U.S. dollar export price index and prices that actual arm's-length foreign customers pay for U.S. goods.

## The Limited Role of Arbitrage

The threat of "grey" markets referred to by the interviewee at the optical products company merits discussion. The interviewee noted that an important factor limiting his firm's ability to separate markets was the threat of arbitrage. To give a flavor of the pressure this could create, he gave an example:

> We recently went to China and as an entry strategy were pricing low. To our chagrin we discovered that this stuff was showing up in various other markets and we were losing our margins there.
> So grey markets are a very important factor in our pricing.

Arbitrage has long held a central place in international economics. It is the bedrock of the "law of one price." But it has also been tapped to shed light on the apparent "puzzle" in U.S. export pricing. One study that asks why American firms price to market less than Japanese firms reaches the conclusion that "it may be because pricing to market is more difficult for American firms to carry out without encouraging grey markets for the products. Third parties in the U.S. market may be better able to take advantage of arbitrage opportunities, which are created when different prices are charged for exports and domestic products."[11] But, as argued in chapter 2, arbitrage has traditionally been a weak "master," and firms have not been obedient "servants." Empirical studies (see chapter 2) have shown that American firms are no exception.

It is therefore not surprising that even the interviewee at the optical products firm went on to note that his firm was able successfully to stem the pressure that arbitrage brought:

> Now it is true that to the extent we can, we do put pressure on our dealers to not engage in this sort of transshipping. For instance, we may not have the inventory they need when they need it if we think these people are engaged in the grey market trade.
> Due to this, and our position in the market and our relationships with most of our dealers and distributors, we are able to stem this grey market business and maintain our local currency prices. . . .
> [Besides] the grey market is less important in the nonconsumer market. For example, if we are engaged in a bid to supply some big

[customer] in Japan . . . and we are competing against [our Japanese competitor], the grey market situation isn't such a problem. So here, we can shade our bid when the dollar moves favorably for us and try and outcompete [the Japanese supplier]. If we all started out at ¥100 per unit, say, and the dollar drops by 40 percent, then we could arguably take our bid down to ¥60. But we will never go to ¥60! We don't really know [our competitor's cost] position in detail, but we have a good intuitive sense. And so if we know that they will be willing to go as low as ¥80 because this is an important deal, then we will bid ¥79.

This situation is a win-win for us whether we get the bid or not. If we get the bid, then we make a good profit, but even if we don't, we have made sure that [our Japanese competitor] loses money, which, in turn, puts them under pressure in the future. It reduces their discretion to invest.

The whole issue is market power. If you are in a position like ours . . . then you can manage your pricing.

These comments are consistent with the evidence uncovered by David Sharp: "It was usually the case that cross-hauling was unimportant, and domestic prices were higher than export or overseas prices."[12] Not only did Sharp find that price *levels* were different across markets, he also found that firms changed their price *relatives* (between export and domestic prices) when the exchange rate changed. Such behavior clearly qualified as pricing to market.[13]

When Sharp asked his interviewees how their firms managed to keep markets separate, the responses he elicited were not dissimilar to those from the optical products company executive:

Just pure dealer loyalty and our kind of gentlemen's agreement to follow the terms of the dealer agreement. The dealer agreement does not . . . we cannot specify some of these things in an agreement, or it would be in restraint of trade. . . . The dealers have done very, very well over the years with us and are reluctant to disturb the chance of renewing their dealer contract.[14]

Noting that they had encountered problems in the past, the interviewee went on to give an unusual account of how they solved their problem: "We would have [products] appearing in Singapore from our Japanese factories. So we, in effect, put in port patrols checking exports, serial numbers. We would try to see what the serial numbers were on the [products] in Singapore and in the storage yards to determine what circumvented route they had followed to get there."[15]

From these excerpts, it would appear that in imperfectly competitive markets (where the bulk of American exports are made), dealer "loyalty" can be created or coaxed through subtle but real pressure from manufacturers in the form of blacklists and credible threats of poor service or future stock-outs. While such pressure may not deter all would-be arbitrageurs, the ten firms in Sharp's sample and the three in this one seem content to plug the major leaks in their price and distribution mechanism. The sentiment is captured well by one of Sharp's interviewees at an office automation company: "If a few guys make a bit of money doing it, well, good luck to them, but we are not going to run our pricing strategy on the basis of what those few guys made. Our thought was to get it right for the bulk of the business."[16]

At a minimum, these anecdotes suggest that arbitrage plays a limited role in preventing American firms from price-discriminating across markets. In conjunction with the empirical studies cited in chapter 2, they indicate that scholars looking to arbitrage to explain their puzzling finding that American firms do not price to market will discover that their explanations are not supported by the evidence.

## Firm Sourcing Responses

Because of the limited duration of the interviews, sourcing issues were given lower priority. But managers were asked to comment on whether, and how, their firms responded in their sourcing to the recent exchange rate changes.

Since each had a different network of worldwide production capabilities, their responses on sourcing were not as unanimous as they were on pricing. Nonetheless, none of the responses was inconsistent with the theoretical and empirical treatment in chapter 3. The response of the officer at the machinery company was most in keeping with the conclusions reached in chapter 3:

> In a strong dollar environment, if we can produce overseas, then we will move our production overseas and turn down U.S. capacity utilization. If we don't have capacity overseas, then we will look to outsource. In any event, we will reduce the value added we do in the U.S.
>
> The opposite is true in a weak dollar environment. We incorporate our forecasts of exchange rates in our five-year plans and we are constantly trying to optimize the use of our capacity across various international locations.
>
> So our U.S.-content level is quite sensitive to the dollar's exchange rate.

At the telecommunications equipment firm, things were slightly different because the firm had no overseas manufacturing operations. But here, too, the officer said that exchange rates affected sourcing decisions:

> While we don't have any manufacturing foreign direct investment, international outsourcing is key for us. In 1985, about 75 percent of our content was U.S. sourced. But during the latter half of the 1980s, as the dollar fell, our U.S. content rose. We brought back to the United States the parts we were sourcing overseas. Today almost 100 percent of our sourcing is U.S.

At the optical products company, the interviewee explained that the company's foreign manufacturing facilities were somewhat specialized. Capacity in various countries was not always fungible, and even if it were, decisions to switch sourcing were taken in light of global profit maximization goals:

Suppose our facility in England purchased [a particular input] from our plant in [the United States] for 30¢ a unit, and for some reason we have decided we would like to have full capacity in [the U.S. plant], then even if the price of [this input] drops in the outside market, say, because the dollar rose, and [our sub in] England wanted to switch [sourcing], we may say no to them. We make this decision on the basis of overall profitability analysis whereas the U.K. manager is maximizing his U.K. profits.

But, yes, this does mean that there is a crossover point in the analysis when we will shift. If there is a large swing in the exchange rate, say, and the relative price of the procured input changes sharply, then company profits may be maximized by idling a portion of the [U.S.] plant and switching sourcing. And we would do this.

This example illustrates the concept of exchange rate "thresholds" developed in chapter 3: that is, the fixed costs that multinational enterprises have to carry in maintaining plants on both sides of the exchange rate may induce them to set an elevated threshold that the exchange rate has to cross before they decide to switch sourcing. From the description given by the interviewee, this notion seems to apply quite well at the optical products company.

## Conclusion

The interview findings indicate quite strongly that the hypotheses advanced in this study hold up better than their rivals. To be sure, this appendix has barely scratched the surface from an organizational standpoint. Fortunately, the processes by which managers with discrete functional responsibilities in the parent office coordinate their pricing and sourcing strategies and actions with their counterparts in foreign subsidiaries is getting new attention.[17] Such research will be indispensable in elucidating the ways in which large enterprises possessing different capabilities and organizational structures respond to cross-cutting exogenous shifts in their competitive environments.

# *Notes*

## Chapter 1

1. In fact, the output of their foreign affiliates alone accounted for about 3 percent of output outside the United States. See Robert E. Lipsey, Magnus Bloomstrom, and Eric D. Ramstetter, "Internationalized Production in World Output," in Robert E. Baldwin, Robert E. Lipsey, and J. David Richardson, eds., *Geography and Ownership as Bases for Economic Accounting*, pp. 83–138 (University of Chicago Press, 1998), p. 87.

2. The share of U.S. multinationals in world GDP declined from 9.2 percent in 1977 to 7.2 percent in 1989. The product of U.S. foreign affiliates was equal to 8.2 percent of U.S. GDP in 1977 and 5.7 percent of U.S. GDP in 1993. See Lipsey and others, "Internationalized Production in World Output," p. 87.

3. In 1993 foreign-owned firms accounted for 15.2 percent of U.S. manufacturing GDP, compared with 4.8 percent in 1974.

4. William J. Zeile, "U.S. Intrafirm Trade in Goods," *Survey of Current Business*, February 1997, pp. 23–38.

5. We take the term "borderless world" from Keniche Ohmae, *The Borderless World* (London: Collins, 1990). According to Ohmae, regions that

span national borders are often more integrated than individual nation-states.

6. Mordechai E. Kreinin, "How Closed Is Japan's Market? Additional Evidence," *World Economy,* vol. 11 (December 1988), pp. 529–42. See also Edward M. Graham and Paul R. Krugman, *Foreign Direct Investment in the United States,* 3d ed. (Washington, D.C.: Institute for International Economics, 1995); William J. Zeile, "The Domestic Orientation of Production and Sales by U.S. Manufacturing Affiliates of Foreign Companies," *Survey of Current Business,* April 1998, pp. 29–50.

7. For a provocative discussion of this subject, see Robert B. Reich, "Who Is Us?" *Harvard Business Review,* vol. 64 (January-February 1990), pp. 53–64. Reich challenges the notion that firms are driven by patriotism rather than profits. He finds deep flaws in the implicit assumption that national governments would advance their own interests by promoting the interests of firms headquartered in their economies.

8. See Paul Krugman, "Increasing Returns, Imperfect Competition and the Positive Theory of International Trade," in Gene M. Grossman and Kenneth Rogoff, eds., *Handbook of International Economics,* vol. 3 (Amsterdam: Elsevier, 1995).

9. See, for example, Richard O'Brien, *Global Financial Integration: The End of Geography,* Chatham House Papers (London: Royal Institute of International Affairs, 1992); Krugman, "Increasing Returns"; Edward E. Leamer and James Levinsohn, "International Trade Theory: The Evidence," in Grossman and Rogoff, *Handbook of International Economics.*

10. In fact, much of the literature suggests that borders still do matter. For explicit models of trade barriers, see Gary C. Hufbauer and Kimberly A. Elliot, *Measuring the Costs of Protection in the United States* (Washington, D.C.: Institute for International Economics, 1994). Gravity models can be found in John McCallum, "National Borders Matter: Canada-U.S. Regional Trade Patterns," *American Economic Review,* vol. 85 (June 1995), pp. 615–23; Shang-Jin Wei, "Intra-National versus International Trade: How Stubborn Are Nations in Global Integration?" Working Paper 5531 (Cambridge, Mass.: National Bureau of Economic Research, 1996); and J. Helliwell, *How Much Do National Borders Matter?* (Brookings, 1998). On measures of international price gaps, see Michael M. Knetter, "Why Are Retail Prices in Japan So High? Evidence from German Export Prices," Working Paper 4894 (Cambridge, Mass.: National Bureau of Economic Research, 1994). On

purchasing power parity, see Kenneth Rogoff, "The Purchasing Power Parity Puzzle," *Journal of Economic Literature,* vol. 34 (June 1996), pp. 647–68. According to Charles Engel and J. H. Rogers, "How Wide Is the Border?" *American Economic Review,* vol. 86 (December 1996), pp. 1112–25, variation for equidistant cities in different countries is much greater than within the same country. David C. Parsley and Shang-Jin Wei, "Convergence to the Law of One Price without Trade Barriers or Currency Fluctuations," *Quarterly Journal of Economics,* vol. 111 (November 1996), pp. 1211–36, find international departures from purchasing power parity are much greater and more long lasting than those among U.S. cities. See also McCallum, "National Borders Matter"; Roger H. Gordon and A. Lans Bovenberg, "Why Is Capital So Immobile Internationally? Possible Explanations and Implications for Capital Income Taxation," *American Economic Review,* vol. 86 (December 1996), pp. 1057–75.

11. Helen B. Junz and Rudolf R. Rhomberg, "Price Competitiveness in Export Trade among Industrial Countries," *American Economic Review,* vol. 63, Papers and Proceedings (May 1973), pp. 412–18; Paul R. Krugman and Richard E. Baldwin, "The Persistence of the U.S. Trade Deficit," *Brookings Papers on Economic Activity,* no. 1 (1987), pp. 1–43.

12. As emphasized by Michael Porter, "Creating Tomorrow's Advantages," in Rowan Gibson, ed., *Rethinking the Future: Rethinking Principles, Competition, Customers, Control, Power, and the World* (Sonoma, Calif.: Nicholas Brealey, 1997), p. 57: "The presence of so many global markets and companies has essentially nullified the advantage of globalness per se. . . . This new phase of globalization is paradoxically putting a greater and greater premium on what I call the 'home base'—the unique critical mass of skill, expertise, suppliers and local institutions that makes certain locations the innovation centers in a particular business."

13. Bruce Kogut, "Foreign Direct Investment as a Sequential Process," in Charles P. Kindleberger and David B. Audtresch, eds., *The Multinational Corporation in the 1980s* (Cambridge, Mass.: MIT Press, 1983); Kogut, "Designing Global Strategies: Profiting from Operational Flexibility," *Sloan Management Review,* vol. 27 (1985), pp. 27–38.

14. Dani Rodrik, *Has Globalization Gone Too Far?* (Washington D.C.: Institute for International Economics, 1997).

15. For a discussion of the concerns about multinationals, see Raymond Vernon, *In the Hurricane's Eye: The Troubled Prospects of Multinational Enter-*

*prise* (Harvard University Press, 1998). For a statement of the case, see Gary Burtless and others, *Globaphobia: Confronting Fears of Open Trade* (Brookings, 1998).

16. For a review of FDI policies, see Theodore H. Moran, *Foreign Direct Investment and Development: The New Policy Agenda for Developing Countries and Economies in Transition* (Washington, D.C.: Institute for International Economics, 1998).

17. See Paul R. Krugman, "Adjustment in the World Economy," in Paul R. Krugman, *Currencies and Crises* (Cambridge, Mass.: MIT Press, 1992), chap. 1.

# Chapter 2

1. Note that this statement holds on average. For studies using disaggregated data, see, for example, Peter Hooper and Catherine L. Mann, "Exchange Rate Pass-Through in the 1980s: The Case of U.S. Imports of Manufactures," *Brookings Papers on Economic Activity*, 1: 1989, pp. 297–329; Richard C. Marston, "Price Behavior in Japanese and U.S. Manufacturing," in Paul R. Krugman, ed., *Trade with Japan: Has the Door Opened Wider?* pp. 121–41 (University of Chicago Press, 1991). These authors find evidence that in some industries U.S. firms do not fully pass exchange rate changes through into export prices.

2. See Paul Krugman and Richard E. Baldwin, "The Persistence of the U.S. Trade Deficit," *Brookings Papers on Economic Activity*, 1: 1987, pp. 1–43.

3. See Hooper and Mann, "Exchange Rate Pass-Through in the 1980s"; Krugman and Baldwin, "The Persistence of the U.S. Trade Deficit."

4. See Robert Z. Lawrence, "U.S. Current Account Adjustment: An Appraisal," *Brookings Papers on Economic Activity*, no. 2 (1990), pp. 343–92; Paul R. Krugman, *Has the Adjustment Process Worked?* Policy Analysis in International Economics 34 (Washington, D.C.: Institute for International Economics, 1991).

5. Paul R. Krugman, "Pricing to Market When the Exchange Rate Changes," in Sven W. Arndt and David J. Richardson, eds., *Real-Financial Linkages among Open Economies*, pp. 49–70 (Cambridge, Mass: MIT Press, 1987).

6. Robert C. Feenstra, "Symmetric Pass-Through of Tariffs and Exchange Rates under Imperfect Competition: An Empirical Test," *Journal of International Economics*, vol. 27 (August 1989), p. 29.

7. Richard C. Marston, "Pricing to Market in Japanese Manufacturing," *Journal of International Economics*, vol. 29 (November 1990), pp. 217–36.

8. On market share and demand dynamics, see Kenneth A. Froot and Paul D. Klemperer, "Exchange Rate Pass-Through When Market Share Matters," *American Economic Review*, vol. 79 (September 1989), pp. 637–54; Kenneth Kasa, "Adjustment Costs and Pricing-to-Market: Theory and Evidence," *Journal of International Economics*, vol. 32 (February 1992), pp. 1–30. On sunk costs, supply-side dynamics, and hysteresis, see Richard E. Baldwin, "Hysteresis in Import Prices: The Beachhead Effect," *American Economic Review*, vol. 78 (September 1988), pp. 773–85; Avinash Dixit, "Hysteresis, Import Penetration, and Exchange Rate Pass-Through," *Quarterly Journal of Economics*, vol. 104 (May 1989), pp. 205–28. On strategic behavior in oligopolistic markets, see Rudiger Dornbusch, "Exchange Rates and Prices," *American Economic Review*, vol. 77 (March 1987), pp. 93–106; Hooper and Mann, "Exchange Rate Pass-Through in the 1980s"; Michael M. Knetter, "Price Discrimination by U.S. and German Exporters," *American Economic Review*, vol. 79 (March 1989), pp. 198–210; Krugman, "Pricing to Market When the Exchange Rate Changes." And on responses to temporary misalignments, see Marston, "Price Behavior in Japanese and U.S. Manufacturing."

9. Kenichi Ohno, "Exchange Rate Fluctuations, Pass-Through, and Market Share," *International Monetary Fund Staff Papers*, vol. 37 (June 1990), pp. 294–310.

10. See Hooper and Mann, "Exchange Rate Pass-Through in the 1980s"; Knetter, "Price Discrimination by U.S. and German Exporters"; and Robert Z. Lawrence, "American Manufacturing in the 1990s: The Adjustment Challenge," in Kenneth W. Chilton, Melinda E. Warren, and Murray L. Weidenbaum, eds., *American Manufacturing in a Global Market* (Boston: Kluwer Academic, 1990).

11. See Marston, "Price Behavior in Japanese and U.S. Manufacturing."

12. Michael M. Knetter, "International Comparisons of Pricing-to-Market Behavior," *American Economic Review*, vol. 83 (June 1993), pp. 473–86.

13. See Robert E. Lipsey, Linda Molinari, and Irving B. Kravis, "Measures of Prices and Price Competitiveness in International Trade in Manu-

factured Goods," in Peter Hooper and J. David Richardson, eds., *International Economic Transactions: Issues in Measurement and Empirical Research,* pp. 144–95 (University of Chicago Press, 1991); Robert E. Lipsey, "The Data Infrastructure for International Economic Research: A Selective Survey," revised version of a paper prepared for the Annual Meeting of the American Economic Association, 1993.

14. Irving B. Kravis and Robert E. Lipsey, *Price Competitiveness in World Trade: A Conference Report of the National Bureau of Economic Research* (New York: National Bureau of Economic Research, 1971).

15. In fact, the BLS export price index, which is based on the *unweighted* responses of more than 2,000 firms, probably gives a disproportionate weight to small firms that are subject to "menu costs" and likely to charge their foreign buyers their U.S. dollar prices.

16. Donald H. Lessard and Srilata Zaheer, "Breaking the Silos: Distributed Knowledge and Strategic Responses to Volatile Exchange Rates," *Strategic Management Journal,* vol. 17, no. 7 (1996), pp. 513–33.

17. Anecdotal evidence also suggests that U.S. firms do not pass through in the way the export price data suggest. See, for example, Ferdinand Protzman, "Why a Lower Dollar Didn't Work," *New York Times,* December 1, 1992, p. D1. Protzman argues that U.S. exports did not get cheaper and imports dearer. See also Andrew Pollack, "In Yen Windfall, U.S. Companies Prefer Profits," *New York Times,* May 5, 1993, p. D1.

18. For intrafirm trade figures, see chapter 1, table 1-1.

19. Similarly, those using conventional terms-of-trade measures to gauge the effects of trade on U.S. national welfare are using an inaccurate measure.

20. Of course, destinations might offer different opportunities for reporting taxes. However, this premium on the shadow price is not likely to be changed in response to exchange rate changes.

21. William Alterman, "Price Trends in U.S. Trade: New Data, New Insights," in Hooper and Richardson, *International Economic Transactions,* p. 128.

22. We are grateful to Terrence Burnham for suggesting the use of this ratio.

23. See Jack Hirshleifer, "On the Economics of Transfer Pricing," *Journal of Business,* vol. 29 (1956), pp. 172–84; Lorraine Eden, "The Microeconomics of Transfer Pricing," in Alan M. Rugman and Lorraine Eden, eds., *Multinationals and Transfer Pricing,* pp. 13–46 (New York: St. Martin's Press,

1985); W. E. Diewert, "Transfer Pricing and Economic Efficiency," in Rugman and Eden, *Multinationals and Transfer Pricing*, pp. 47–81; and Ralph L. Benke, Jr., and James Don Edwards, *Transfer Pricing: Techniques and Uses* (New York: National Association of Accountants, 1980), appendix B.

24. Alterman, "Price Trends in U.S. Trade," p. 137. Emphasis added.

25. See Lipsey, "The Data Infrastructure for International Economic Research."

26. See Thomas Horst, "Theory of the Multinational Firm: Optimal Behavior under Differing Tariff and Tax Rates," *Journal of Political Economy*, vol. 79 (September/October 1971), pp. 1059–72; Feenstra, "Symmetric Pass-Through of Tariffs and Exchange Rates under Imperfect Competition."

27. "Top 50 U.S. Exporters," *Fortune*, Summer-Spring 1991, p. 59; *Trade & Employment*, 3d Quarter, March 1992, table 5.

28. Authors' calculations using Standard & Poor's, *Compustat* CD-ROM, February 1992. See also Subramanian Rangan, "The Pricing and Sourcing Responses of U.S. Multinationals to Exchange Rate Changes," Ph.D. Dissertation, Harvard University, Kennedy School of Government and Graduate School of Arts and Sciences, 1994.

29. U.S. Department of Commerce, Bureau of Economic Analysis, *U.S. Direct Investment Abroad: 1989 Benchmark Survey: Preliminary Results* (hereafter *USDIA: 1989*), 1991, table 85, col. 1; *Trade & Employment*, 3d Quarter, March 1992, table 5.

30. See table 1-1. For purposes of evaluating the foreign market pricing responses of U.S. firms even this number may be an underestimate. Catherine Mann, personal communication. She notes that an increasing proportion of U.S. exports will make a round-trip back to the United States since they are sent abroad by U.S. firms to foreign enterprises that assemble or add value to the exported products and then ship them back to the U.S. firm. In such instances, she notes, there is little incentive for the U.S. firm to price such "exports" strategically.

31. *USDIA: 1989*, table 85, col. 14, excludes "other transportation."

32. *USDIA: 1989*, table 85, cols. 5 and 13; table 41, col. 9.

33. See Michael Waterson, *Economic Theory of the Industry* (Cambridge University Press, 1984), esp. chap. 2; also appendix A of this book.

34. For oligopolists, the price-cost margin will be equal to

$$\frac{\sum s_i^2 (1 + \lambda_i)}{-\eta} = \frac{H}{\eta} (1 + \mu),$$

where $H$ is the Herfindahl index of concentration, $\mu$ is the weighted sum of the conjectural variations of each firm about the output responses of all other firms in the industry, and $\eta$ is the industry price elasticity of demand. See Waterson, *Economic Theory of the Industry*, pp. 19–20. In monopoly situations, $PCM_i = 1/-\eta$, and in Cournot competition, $PCM_i = H/-\eta$.

35. That other (more convex) demand schedules are less plausible has been shown by Feenstra, "Symmetric Pass-Through of Tariffs and Exchange Rates under Imperfect Competition," p. 29. See also Marston, "Pricing to Market in Japanese Manufacturing," p. 221; Michael M. Knetter, "Multinationals and Pricing to Market Behavior," in Michael W. Klein and Paul J. J. Welfens, eds., *Multinationals in the New Europe and Global Trade* (New York: Springer-Verlag, 1992), p. 69.

36. The term "pricing to market" is from Krugman, "Pricing to Market When the Exchange Rate Changes." Management scholars have something similar in mind when they argue that "it is important to realize that prices are constrained by market structure, competitive rivalry and competitors' strategic intentions in a given market and not [just] by cost to the firm." C. K. Prahalad and Yves L. Doz, *The Multinational Mission: Balancing Local Demands and Global Vision* (New York: The Free Press, 1987), p. 46.

37. See Hooper and Mann, "Exchange Rate Pass-Through in the 1980s."

38. An exercise along these lines is presented in Rangan, "Pricing and Sourcing Responses of U.S. Multinationals to Exchange Rate Changes," which reaches conclusions similar to those presented here.

39. Country coverage is limited by the fact that the Department of Commerce reports industry by country data for only these nine countries (Canada, France, Germany, Netherlands, Italy, Switzerland, United Kingdom, Australia, and Japan). Together, they accounted for 74 percent of the $500 billion worth of sales that U.S. majority-owned foreign affiliates in manufacturing made worldwide in 1989. See *USDIA: 1989, Preliminary Results*, table 33.

40. It must be acknowledged that, as specified, this equation constrains the exchange rate coefficient to be the same across all industries. This is done to conserve degrees of freedom. In fact, firms in different manufacturing industries are likely to show different propensities to price to market, depending on the shape of the demand curves they face, the importance of sunk costs, and market share. See Krugman, "Pricing to Market When the Exchange Rate Changes"; Rudiger Dornbusch, "Exchange Rates and Prices," *American Economic Review*, vol. 77 (March 1987), pp. 93–106.

41. The starting date of 1982 (as opposed to, say, 1980) is dictated by the availability of data: U.S. Department of Commerce data on the operations of U.S. multinationals are not available for 1980 and 1981.

42. See Waterson, *Economic Theory of the Industry,* pp. 19–20; Ian R. Domowitz, R. Glenn Hubbard, and Bruce C. Petersen, "Oligopoly Supergames: Some Empirical Evidence on Prices and Margins," *Journal of Industrial Economics,* vol. 35 (June 1987), pp. 383–85. See also Domowitz, Hubbard, and Petersen, "Market Structure and Cyclical Fluctuations in U.S. Manufacturing," *Review of Economics and Statistics,* vol. 70 (February 1988), p. 58, in which the authors conclude that this assumption (which is routinely made in the literature to get around the lack of data on marginal costs) is empirically tenable.

43. See Domowitz and others, "Oligopoly Supergames," pp. 379–98.

44. See Pinelopi K. Goldberg, "Product Differentiation and Oligopoly in International Markets: The Case of the U.S. Automobile Industry," *Econometrica,* vol. 63 (July 1995), pp. 891–951.

45. See Knetter, "Multinationals and Pricing to Market Behavior," p. 68.

46. The $F$-test for equality of coefficients was conducted after pretesting for equality of variances. G. S. Maddala, *Introduction to Econometrics* (New York: Macmillan, 1992), p. 177. The null hypothesis on the Chow test for stability could not be rejected at the 5 percent level.

47. See Alterman, "Price Trends in U.S. Trade"; Hooper and Mann, "Exchange Rate Pass-Through in the 1980s"; Marston, "Price Behavior in Japanese and U.S. Manufacturing"; Michael H. Moffett, "The *J*-Curve Revisited: An Empirical Examination for the United States," *Journal of International Money and Finance,* vol. 8 (September 1989), pp. 425–44.

48. See Pinelopi K. Goldberg and M. M. Knetter, "Goods Prices and Exchange Rates: What Have We Learned?" *Journal of Economic Literature,* vol. 35 (September 1997), pp. 1243–72.

## Chapter 3

1. See, for example, Raymond Vernon, "International Investment and International Trade in the Product Cycle," *Quarterly Journal of Economics* 80 (May 1966), pp. 190–207; Mira Wilkins, *The Maturing of Multinational*

*Enterprise: American Business Abroad from 1914 to 1970* (Harvard University Press, 1974); Bruce Kogut, "Foreign Direct Investment as a Sequential Process," in Charles P. Kindleberger and David B. Audtresch, eds., *The Multinational Corporation in the 1980s*, pp. 38–56 (MIT Press, 1983); Bruce Kogut, "Designing Global Strategies: Profiting from Operational Flexibility," *Sloan Management Review*, vol. 27 (1985), pp. 27–38; John H. Dunning and Alan M. Rugman, "The Influence of Hymer's Dissertation on the Theory of Foreign Direct Investment," *American Economic Review*, vol. 75 (May 1985), pp. 228–32; Michael E. Porter, ed., *Competition in Global Industries* (Harvard Business School Press, 1986), esp. the chapter by Donald R. Lessard, "Finance and Global Competition: Exploiting Financial Scope and Coping with Volatile Exchange Rates," pp. 147–84; Sumantra Ghoshal, "Global Strategy: An Organizing Framework," *Strategic Management Journal*, vol. 8 (1987), pp. 425–40; Richard E. Caves, *Multinational Enterprise and Economic Analysis*, 2d ed. (Cambridge University Press, 1996).

2. Dunning and Rugman, "The Influence of Hymer's Dissertation," p. 230.

3. Kogut, "Foreign Direct Investment as a Sequential Process," "Designing Global Strategies: Profiting from Operational Flexibility," and "A Note on Global Strategies," *Strategic Management Journal*, vol. 10 (1989), pp. 383–89; Bruce Kogut and Nalin Kulatilaka, "Operating Flexibility, Global Manufacturing, and the Option Value of a Multinational Network," *Management Science*, vol. 40 (January 1994), pp. 123–39; Peter J. Buckley and Mark C. Casson, "Models of the Multinational Enterprise," *Journal of International Business Studies*, vol. 29, no. 1 (1998), pp. 21–44; Donald R. Lessard and John B. Lightstone, "Volatile Exchange Rates Can Put Operations at Risk," *Harvard Business Review*, vol. 64 (July-August 1986), pp. 107–14; Ghoshal, "Global Strategy."

4. Kogut, "Designing Global Strategies."

5. Kogut, "A Note on Global Strategies," p. 387.

6. Linda Allen and Christos Pantzalis, "Valuation of the Operating Flexibility of Multinational Corporations," *Journal of International Business Studies*, vol. 27, no. 4 (1996), pp. 633–53.

7. Jane S. Little, "Intra-Firm Trade: An Update," *New England Economic Review* (May–June 1987), pp. 46–51.

8. Kogut, "Foreign Direct Investment as a Sequential Process," and "Designing Global Strategies."

9. David Besanko, David Dranove, and Mark Shanley, *The Economics of Strategy* (John Wiley, 1996), p. 502.

10. It is, therefore, not meaningful to discuss distinctions between temporary and permanent exchange rate changes. See Kenneth A. Froot and Richard H. Thaler, "Anomalies: Foreign Exchange," *Journal of Economic Perspectives*, vol. 4 (Summer 1990), pp. 179–92.

11. Kogut and Kulatilaka, "Operating Flexibility."

12. Stephen H. Hymer, *The International Operations of National Firms: A Study of Direct Investment* (MIT Press, 1976).

13. Sumantra Ghoshal and Nitin Nohria, "Internal Differentiation within Multinational Corporations," *Strategic Management Journal*, vol. 10 (July 1989), pp. 323–37.

14. Oliver E. Williamson, *Markets and Hierarchies, Analysis and Antitrust Implications: A Study in the Economics of Internal Organization* (New York: The Free Press, 1975), pp. 119–25.

15. Thomas H. Johnson and Robert S. Kaplan, *Relevance Lost: The Rise and Fall of Management Accounting* (Harvard Business School Press, 1987).

16. Arthur L. Stinchcombe, "Social Structure and Organizations," in James G. March, ed., *Handbook of Organizations*, pp. 142–93 (Chicago: Rand McNally, 1965).

17. Christopher A. Bartlett and Sumantra Ghoshal, *Managing across Borders: The Transnational Solution* (Harvard Business School Press, 1989), p. 81.

18. David J. Collis, "A Resource-Based Analysis of Global Competition: The Case of the Bearings Industry," *Strategic Management Journal*, vol. 12, Special Issue (Summer 1991), p. 53.

19. Robert A. Jones and Joseph M. Ostroy, "Flexibility and Uncertainty," *Review of Economic Studies*, vol. 51 (January 1984), p. 16.

20. In a 1939 article, George Stigler "describes one plant as being more flexible than another if it has a flatter average cost curve" (cited in Jones and Ostroy, *Flexibility and Uncertainty*, p. 25). Indeed, the flexibility investments described above would take firms in precisely this direction.

21. John H. Dunning, *Multinational Enterprise and the Global Economy* (Workingham, England: Addison-Wesley, 1993), p. 117; Wilkins, *The Maturing of Multinational Enterprise*, pp. 434–35.

22. John Stopford and Louis T. Wells, Jr., *Managing the Multinational Enterprise: Organization of the Firm and Ownership of the Subsidiaries* (New York: Basic Books, 1972); Bartlett and Ghoshal, *Managing across Borders*, p. 46.

23. Dunning, *Multinational Enterprise and the Global Economy*; Wilkins, *The Maturing of Multinational Enterprise,* chap. 14; Bartlett and Ghoshal, *Managing across Borders,* p. 46

24. Louis T. Wells, Jr., *Conflict or Indifference: U. S. Multinationals in a World of Regional Trading Blocs,* OECD Technical Paper 57 (Paris: Organization for Economic Cooperation and Development, 1992).

25. Paul Einzig, *The History of Foreign Exchange* (London: Macmillan, 1970).

26. In arm's-length markets, the actual extent of pass-through will depend on the price elasticities of demand in the home and foreign markets, the relative sizes of the two markets, the slope of producers' marginal cost curves, and the degree of competition in the market. See Michael M. Knetter, "International Comparisons of Pricing-to-Market Behavior," *American Economic Review,* vol. 83 (June 1993), pp. 473–86. In the intrafirm case, changes in MNEs' transfer prices ought to reflect changes in marginal costs. See Lessard, "Finance and Global Competition," pp. 147–84.

27. Of all U.S. exports made to manufacturing MOFAs, more than 90 percent originate from the U.S. parent (that is, intrafirm trade), and typically less than 20 percent of the total is intended "for resale without further manufacture." In other words, the vast majority are intermediate products. U.S. Department of Commerce, Bureau of Economic Analysis, *U.S. Direct Investment Abroad* [hereafter *USDIA*], various years, tables III.H.5, III.H.9, and III.H.15. These proportions are fairly stable over the time period covered in this study.

28. $t - k$ could encompass an interval of one or, as in the case of a prolonged episode, several years.

29. Morris Goldstein and Moshin S. Khan, "Income and Price Effects in Foreign Trade," in Ronald W. Jones and Peter B. Kenen, eds., *Handbook of International Economics,* vol. 2, pp. 1041–1105 (Amsterdam: Elsevier, 1984).

30. Goldstein and Khan, "Income and Price Effects in Foreign Trade."

31. Lawrence G. Franko, *The European Multinationals: A Renewed Challenge for American and British Big Business* (Harper & Row, 1976); Bartlett and Ghoshal, *Managing across Borders.*

32. Besanko and others, *The Economics of Strategy,* p. 502; Kogut and Kulatilaka, "Operating Flexibility."

33. Using levels rather than changes in capacity utilization does not alter the findings. Also, simple calculations using U.S. and OECD data on manufacturing capacity utilization do not support the capacity limits story.

For instance, between 1985 and 1993, when the dollar tumbled and stayed low (see figure 3-1), U.S. manufacturing capacity utilization averaged 80.6 percent (*Economic Report of the President*, 1994, table B-52, p. 327). The reported highs for capacity utilization in 1973 and 1966 were 88.1 and 91.1 percent, respectively. Rough estimates based on U.S. manufacturing GDP (*Economic Report of the President*, 1994, table B-12, p. 283) suggest that the productive capacity contained in these extra seven to ten percentage points of capacity was between $70 and $100 billion. Compare those figures with the possible demands of the European and Japanese affiliates of U.S. MNEs. In 1985, when the dollar was at its peak and U.S. content was very expensive, the value of U.S. inputs used by these affiliates was running at just around $10 billion (*USDIA: 1985*, table 52). If this figure had risen to $30 or $40 billion, U.S. capacity utilization would have risen by just two or three percentage points. But eight years later, when the dollar had tumbled by more than 35 percent, the figure had risen to just over $20 billion (*USDIA: 1993*, table III.H.5). The OECD data on manufacturing capacity utilization in European countries tell a similar story. During the early 1980s, when the dollar was high, German and French manufacturing capacity utilization had dropped substantially and was running at well below 80 percent (OECD, *Indicators of Industrial Activity*).

34. Wells, *Conflict or Indifference*, p. 16.

35. Kogut, "Designing Global Strategies."

36. Frederick T. Knickerbocker, *Oligopolistic Reaction and Multinational Enterprise* (Harvard University, Graduate School of Business Administration, Division of Research, 1973); Raymond Vernon, "Organizational and Institutional Responses to International Risk," in Richard J. Herring, ed., *Managing International Risk: Essays Commissioned in Honor of the Centenary of the Wharton School, University of Pennsylvania*, pp. 191–216 (Cambridge University Press, 1983).

37. S. Lael Brainard and David Riker, "Are U.S. Multinationals Exporting U.S. Jobs?" unpublished paper (MIT Sloan School, July 1995); Stephen J. Kobrin, "An Empirical Analysis of the Determinants of Global Integration," *Strategic Management Journal*, vol. 12, Special Issue (Summer 1991), pp. 17–31.

38. Brainard and Riker, "Are U.S. Multinationals Exporting U.S. Jobs?"

39. Jones and Ostroy, "Flexibility and Uncertainty," p. 16.

40. See Paul R. Krugman, ed., *Trade with Japan: Has the Door Opened Wider?* (University of Chicago Press, 1991), especially the chapters by

Robert Z. Lawrence, "How Open Is Japan?" pp. 9–37; and by Peter A. Petri, "Market Structure, Comparative Advantage, and Japanese Trade under the Strong Yen," pp. 51–84.

41. When we replaced the U.S.-in-Japan figures in the pooled regression model 6 by the equivalent Japan-in-the-U.S. figures, the results were nearly identical to those reported in table 3-9. Including a Japan dummy and a Japan dummy and vintage interaction term did not alter the results. (Coefficients on the latter terms were not statistically significant.) These results reinforce our earlier finding that the sourcing behavior of Japanese multinationals in the United States is not different from the behavior of U.S. multinationals abroad.

## Chapter 4

1. See C. Fred Bergsten, Thomas Horst, and Theodore H. Moran, *American Multinationals and American Interests* (Brookings, 1978), esp. chap. 8.

2. See Bergsten and others, *American Multinationals and American Interests*; Richard E. Caves, *Multinational Enterprise and Economic Analysis,* 2d ed. (Cambridge University Press, 1996).

3. See David J. Goldsbrough, "International Trade of Multinational Corporations and Its Responsiveness to Changes in Aggregate Demand and Relative Prices," *International Monetary Fund Staff Papers*, vol. 28 (September 1981), p. 573–99: "Trade flows generated by the location decisions of a firm with large fixed investments in several countries may not respond as rapidly to shifts in relative prices as those of an independent producer . . . unconcerned with the effect of its actions on the profitability of overseas affiliates." Also Gerald K. Helleiner, *Intra-Firm Trade and the Developing Countries* (New York: St. Martin's Press, 1981), p. 3: intrafirm trade "can and usually do[es] take place in consequence of central commands rather than in response to price signals." And Jane S. Little (1986: 46): "Because intra-firm trade is potentially 'managed' trade . . . the pace or size of its adjustment [differs] from that of trade between unaffiliated firms." In addition, see Kang Rae Cho, "The Role of Product-Specific Factors in Intra-Firm Trade of U.S. Manufacturing Multinational Corporations," *Journal of International Business Studies*, vol. 21, no. 2 (1990), pp. 319–30; and Dennis J. Encarnation, *Rivals beyond Trade: America versus Japan in Global Competition* (Cornell University Press, 1992).

4. John McCallum, "National Borders Matter: Canada-U.S. Regional Trade Patterns," *American Economic Review,* vol. 85 (June 1995), pp. 615–23.

5. Shang-Jin Wei, "Intra-National versus International Trade: How Stubborn Are Nations in Global Integration?" Working Paper 5531 (Cambridge, Mass.: National Bureau of Economic Research, 1996).

6. Paul R. Krugman and Richard E. Baldwin, "The Persistence of the U.S. Trade Deficit," *Brookings Papers on Economic Activity*, 1: 1987, pp. 1–43.

7. Gene M. Grossman, Comment on Alan V. Deardorff, "Determinants of Bilateral Trade: Does Gravity Work in a Neoclassical World?" in Jeffrey A. Frankel, ed., *The Regionalization of the World Economy* (University of Chicago Press, 1998), p. 31.

8. Paul R. Krugman, "Increasing Returns, Imperfect Competition and the Positive Theory of International Trade," in Gene M. Grossman and Kenneth Rogoff, eds., *Handbook of International Economics*, vol. 3 (Amsterdam: Elsevier, 1995), p. 1273.

9. Krugman, "Increasing Returns," p. 1273, fn.

10. Frederick E. Webster, Jr., and Yoram Wind, *Organizational Buying Behavior* (Englewood Cliffs, N.J.: Prentice-Hall, 1972); Blair H. Sheppard and Marla Tuchinsky, "Interfirm Relationships: A Grammar of Pairs," in Barry M. Stow and L. L. Cummings, eds., *Research in Organizational Behavior,* vol. 18, pp. 331–73 (Greenwich, Conn.: JAI Press, 1996).

11. David M. Gould, "Immigrant Links to the Home Country: Empirical Implications for U.S. Bilateral Trade Flows," *Review of Economics and Statistics,* vol. 76 (May 1994), p. 303.

12. Mark Granovetter, "Economic Action and Social Structure: The Problem of Embeddedness," *American Journal of Sociology,* vol. 91 (November 1985), pp. 481–510.

13. Neng Liang and Rodney L. Stump, "Judgemental Heuristics in Overseas Vendor Search and Evaluation: A Proposed Model of Importer Buying Behavior," *International Executive,* vol. 38 (November 1996), pp. 779–806; Hokey Min and William P. Galle, "International Purchasing Strategies of Multinational U.S. Firms," *International Journal of Purchasing and Materials Management,* vol. 2 (1991), p. 509.

14. See Ranjay Gulati, "Does Familiarity Breed Trust? The Implications of Repeated Ties for Contractual Choice in Alliances," *Academy of Management Journal,* vol. 38 (February 1995), pp. 85–112; Alejandro Portes and Julia Sensenbrenner, "Embeddedness and Immigration: Notes on the Social

Determinants of Economic Action," *American Journal of Sociology,* vol. 98 (May 1993), pp. 1320–50; Brian Uzzi, "Social Structure and Competition in Interfirm Networks: The Paradox of Embeddedness," *Administrative Science Quarterly,* vol. 42 (March 1997), pp. 35–67.

15. See Webster and Wind, *Organizational Buying Behavior;* Mary Lou Egan and Ashoka Moody, "Buyer-Seller Links in Export Development," *World Development,* vol. 20 (March 1992), pp. 321–34; Gulati, "Does Familiarity Breed Trust?"; Xavier Martin, Will Mitchell, and Anand Swaminathan, "Recreating and Extending Japanese Automobile Buyer-Supplier Links in North America," *Strategic Management Journal,* vol. 16 (November 1995), pp. 589–619; Roger H. Gordon and A. Lans Bovenberg, "Why Is Capital so Immobile Internationally? Possible Explanations and Implications for Capital Income Taxation," *American Economic Review,* vol. 86 (December 1996), pp. 1057–75.

16. Neng Liang and Arvind Parkhe, "Importer Behavior: The Neglected Counterpart of International Exchange," *Journal of International Business Studies,* vol. 28, no. 3 (1997), pp. 510–11.

17. Egan and Moody, "Buyer-Seller Links in Export Development," pp. 321, 325.

18. See Krugman and Baldwin, "The Persistence of the U.S. Trade Deficit"; Robert Z. Lawrence, "U.S. Current Account Adjustment: An Appraisal," *Brookings Papers on Economic Activity,* 2: 1990, pp. 343–92; Charles Engel and John H. Rogers, "How Wide Is the Border?" *American Economic Review,* vol. 86 (December 1996), pp. 1112–25.

19. Bruce Kogut, "Foreign Direct Investment as a Sequential Process," in Charles P. Kindleberger and David B. Audtresch, eds., *The Multinational Corporation in the 1980s,* pp. 38–56 (MIT Press, 1983); Sumantra Ghoshal and Christopher A. Bartlett, "The Multinational Corporation as an Interorganizational Network," *Academy of Management Review,* vol. 15 (October 1990), pp. 603–25.

20. Warren J. Keegan, "Multinational Scanning: A Study of the Information Sources Utilized by Headquarters Executives in Multinational Companies," *Administrative Science Quarterly* (September 1974), p. 414.

21. Anders Edstrom and Jay R. Galbraith, "Transfer of Managers as a Coordination and Control Strategy in Multinational Organizations," *Administrative Science Quarterly,* vol. 22 (1977), pp. 248–63; C. K. Prahalad and Yves L. Doz, *The Multinational Mission: Balancing Local Demands and Global Vision* (New York: The Free Press, 1987); Christopher A. Bartlett

and Sumantra Ghoshal, *Managing across Borders: The Transnational Solution* (Harvard Business School Press, 1989).

22. Raymond Vernon, "The Product Cycle Hypothesis in a New International Environment," *Oxford Bulletin of Economics and Statistics,* vol. 41 (November 1979), pp. 255–67; Kogut, "Foreign Direct Investment as a Sequential Process"; John H. Dunning and Alan M. Rugman, "The Influence of Hymer's Dissertation on the Theory of Foreign Direct Investment," *American Economic Review,* vol. 75 (May 1985), pp. 228–32; Donald R. Lessard, "Finance and Global Competition: Exploiting Financial Scope and Coping with Volatile Exchange Rates," in Michael E. Porter, ed., *Competition in Global Industries* (Harvard Business School Press, 1986), pp. 147–84.

23. Frederick T. Knickerbocker, *Oligopolistic Reaction and Multinational Enterprise* (Harvard University, Graduate School of Business Administration, Division of Research, 1973), p. 26.

24. Keegan, "Multinational Scanning,"; Egan and Moody, "Buyer-Seller Links in Export Development."

25. Robert M. Stern, Jonathan Francis, and Bruce Schumacher, *Price Elasticities in International Trade: An Annotated Bibliography* (London: Macmillan, 1976).

26. George J. Stigler, "The Economics of Information," *Journal of Political Economy,* vol. 69 (June 1961), pp. 213–25.

27. U.S. Department of Commerce, Bureau of Economic Analysis, *U.S. Direct Investment Abroad: 1977 Benchmark Survey,* 1981, tables B and C, and *1994 Benchmark Survey, Preliminary Results,* 1994, tables II.A.1, II.A.2.

28. Raymond Vernon, "International Investment and International Trade in the Product Cycle," *Quarterly Journal of Economics,* vol. 80 (May 1966), pp. 190–207; John H. Dunning, ed., *Economic Analysis and the Multinational Enterprise* (London: Allen and Unwin, 1974); Caves, *Multinational Enterprise and Economic Analysis.*

29. Helen B. Junz and Rudolf R. Rhomberg, "Price Competitiveness in Export Trade among Industrial Countries," *American Economic Review,* vol. 63, Papers and Proceedings (May 1973), pp. 412–18; Lawrence, "U.S. Current Account Adjustment."

30. Oliver E. Williamson, *Markets and Hierarchies, Analysis and Antitrust Implications* (New York: The Free Press, 1975).

31. See John H. Dunning, *Multinational Enterprise and the Global Economy* (Workingham, England: Addison-Wesley, 1993); Stephen J. Kobrin, "An

Empirical Analysis of the Determinants of Global Integration," *Strategic Management Journal,* vol. 12, Special Issue (Summer 1991), pp. 17–31.

32. See William H. Greene, *Econometric Analysis* (New York: Macmillan, 1990), pp. 482–85.

33. The results of these regressions can be found in Subramanian Rangan, "Search and Deliberation in International Exchange: Microfoundations to Some Macro Patterns," INSEAD Working Paper (1999).

34. To explore the "quantum effect," we added the absolute magnitude of the exchange rate change in some of our regressions. This variable did not take a statistically significant coefficient, nor did it change the results. These findings are consistent with those in Morris Goldstein and Moshin S. Khan, "Income and Price Effects in Foreign Trade," in Ronald W. Jones and Peter B. Kenen, eds., *Handbook of International Economics,* vol. 2 (Amsterdam: Elsevier, 1984), pp. 1041–1105. We also acknowledge that exchange rate expectations do not figure in our regressions. We assume all exchange rate changes are "permanent." However, to the extent that expectations about exchange rate are important, we have no reason to believe the MNEs and non-MNEs form systematically different expectations. If the "temporariness" of exchange rate changes might be gauged by the volatility in exchange rate changes, then exchange rate changes do not appear to have become more temporary. Volatility (measured as the standard deviation of monthly percentage changes) in exchange rates of G7 economies during 1980–85, 1986–89, and 1990–94 was 1.7, 1.7, and 1.6 respectively (see *The Economist,* October 7, 1995, Survey, p. 28). So volatility is unlikely to be useful as an independent variable in our regressions.

35. Organization for Economic Cooperation and Development, *Globalisation and Small and Medium Enterprises (SMEs),* vol. 1 (Paris: OECD, 1997), vol. 1, p. 54.

36. Lessard, "Finance and Global Competition."

37. Krugman and Baldwin, "The Persistence of the U.S. Trade Deficit."

38. See Peter J. Williamson, "Multinational Enterprise Behavior and Domestic Industry Adjustment under Import Threat," *Review of Economics and Statistics,* vol. 68 (August 1986), pp, 359–68; Gould, "Immigrant Links to the Home Country"; James E. Rauch, "Networks versus Markets in International Trade," unpublished working paper, Department of Economics, University of California, San Diego, La Jolla, Calif. (August 1997).

39. Some corroboration of these views can be found in Rauch, "Networks versus Markets in International Trade."

40. Again, see Rauch, "Networks versus Markets in International Trade." Rauch reports results that are consistent with these arguments and expectations: "The coefficients on colonial ties are always positive, significant and largest for the differentiated commodity group in every year" (p. 28).

41. See Rauch, "Networks versus Markets in International Trade."

## Appendix A

1. Raymond Vernon, *Sovereignty at Bay: The Multinational Spread of U.S. Enterprises* (New York: Basic Books, 1971).

2. F. M. Scherer, *Industrial Market Structure and Economic Performance*, 2d ed. (Chicago: Rand McNally, 1980), p. 229.

3. Demand conditions are assumed to be such that selling at a high price in just one market is dominated by selling in both markets at a lower uniform price.

4. Richard C. Marston, "Pricing to Market in Japanese Manufacturing," *Journal of International Economics*, vol. 29 (November 1990), p. 221.

5. If the U.S. firm faces capacity constraints, then, naturally, it will not lower its foreign currency prices.

6. Joe Bain (1956) called this "blockaded entry" (see Scherer, *Industrial Market Structure*, p. 237).

7. The U.S. producer will be able to make economic profits assuming that it has no other American competitors with whom it is engaged in Bertrand price competition. Otherwise, pass-through will be complete. Entry by other U.S. firms and limit pricing strategies will also lead to a higher degree of pass-through than otherwise.

8. This is considered by Paul R. Krugman, "Pricing to Market When the Exchange Rate Changes," in Sven W. Arndt and David J. Richardson, eds., *Real-Financial Linkages among Open Economies* (MIT Press, 1987), pp. 60–62.

9. Krugman, "Pricing to Market When the Exchange Rate Changes," p. 62.

10. See Krugman, "Pricing to Market When the Exchange Rate Changes," p. 62.

11. Following Michael Waterson, *Economic Theory of the Industry* (Cambridge University Press, 1984), p. 28.

12. Raymond Vernon, *Sovereignty at Bay: The Multinational Spread of U.S. Enterprises* (New York: Basic Books, 1971).

13. Krugman, "Pricing to Market When the Exchange Rate Changes," p. 65; Kenneth A. Froot and Paul D. Klemperer, "Exchange Rate Pass-Through When Market Share Matters," *American Economic Review*, vol. 79 (September 1989), pp. 637–54. For a detailed discussion of the dynamics of oligopoly pricing, see Scherer, *Industrial Market Structure*, esp. chap. 8.

14. The example is from Krugman, "Pricing to Market When the Exchange Rate Changes," pp. 65–66.

15. Krugman, "Pricing to Market When the Exchange Rate Changes," p. 66.

16. Froot and Klemperer, "Exchange Rate Pass-Through."

17. For simplicity, the interperiod duration is assumed to be one year here. Otherwise, the discount factor should be written as $\rho^i = \beta/(1 + r^i)$, where $\beta$ "measures the duration of the second period relative to the first." See Froot and Klemperer, "Exchange Rate Pass-Through," p. 640.

18. The results do not change if U.S. interest rates are allowed to vary so long as "the interest differential increases" when the exchange rate changes. See Froot and Klemperer, "Exchange Rate Pass-Through," p. 642, esp. fn. 24.

19. Froot and Klemperer, "Exchange Rate Pass-Through," p. 640.

20. Froot and Klemperer, "Exchange Rate Pass-Through," p. 643, fn. 26.

21. Froot and Klemperer, "Exchange Rate Pass-Through," p. 643.

22. Froot and Klemperer, "Exchange Rate Pass-Through," p. 643.

23. Paul Klemperer, "The Competitiveness of Markets with Switching Costs," *Rand Journal of Economics*, vol. 18 (Spring 1987), pp. 149–50.

# Appendix B

1. David J. Sharp, "Control Systems and Decision-Making in Multinational Firms: Price Management under Floating Exchange Rates," Ph.D. dissertation, MIT Sloan School of Management, 1987.

2. Of the officers interviewed, two were presidents, one was a recently retired vice-chairman, two were veteran international sales managers, and one was an assistant treasurer responsible for foreign exchange management.

3. Interestingly, the vice-president of international sales at a leading American winery made much the same point when asked about his firm's *foreign* pricing responses to exchange rate changes. Maintaining the local currency "price position" of his product was crucial to his firm's marketing efforts, he said, since it was customary to signal the quality of wine through price. Beyond undertaking currency hedging, his firm varied its foreign profit margins to stabilize local currency prices. Conversation relayed by F. M. Scherer.

4. Prices are rescaled.

5. Profit-margin movements over the same period at the firm's closest and most direct competitor (a non-U.S. firm) do not show similar patterns. This makes it less likely that industry-wide trends, rather than exchange rates, contributed to the observed movements.

6. Sharp, "Control Systems and Decision-Making in Multinational Firms," p. 183.

7. Sharp, "Control Systems and Decision-Making in Multinational Firms," pp. 183–84.

8. Sharp, "Control Systems and Decision-Making in Multinational Firms," p. 184.

9. Sharp, "Control Systems and Decision-Making in Multinational Firms," p. 197.

10. Sharp, "Control Systems and Decision-Making in Multinational Firms," p. 153.

11. Richard C. Marston, "Price Behavior in Japanese and U.S. Manufacturing," in Paul R. Krugman, ed., *Trade with Japan: Has the Door Opened Wider?* (University of Chicago Press, 1991), p. 139.

12. Sharp, "Control Systems and Decision-Making in Multinational Firms," p. 196.

13. See Marston, "Price Behavior in U.S. and Japanese Manufacturing."

14. Sharp, "Control Systems and Decision-Making in Multinational Firms," p. 199.

15. Sharp, "Control Systems and Decision-Making in Multinational Firms," p. 199.

16. Sharp, "Control Systems and Decision-Making in Multinational Firms," p. 200.

17. See Donald H. Lessard and Srilata Zaheer, "Breaking the Silos: Distributed Knowledge and Strategic Responses to Volatile Exchange Rates," *Strategic Management Journal,* vol. 17, no. 7 (1996), pp. 513–33.

# *Index*

Adjustment processes: activity levels, 107; effects of multinational enterprises on, 5; exchange rates and, 10–11, 49–61, 88; information and, 118; price and income changes, 12, 29–33, 50; stickiness, 13–14, 54–55, 93, 95; trade, 23–25; transaction costs and, 12
Arbitrage, 4, 10, 27
Asia, 81–82, 87
Asia-Pacific Economic Cooperation (APEC), 19
Australia, 82, 103–04, 113
Automobile industry (U.S.), 42

BEA. *See* Bureau of Economic Analysis
Beverage industry, 41, 46

BLS. *See* Bureau of Labor Statistics
Bureau of Economic Analysis (BEA), 46, 61, 64–65, 67, 74, 75, 103
Bureau of Labor Statistics (BLS), 23, 27, 28, 29, 29–33
Business firms, 1, 2
Business issues: border barriers, 118, 119, 121–22; buyer-supplier relationships, 94, 97–98; competition, 3, 4; conglomerate formation, 18; collusion, 3; costs, 4, 6, 9, 38, 44, 45, 72, 95, 97, 107; information discontinuities, 13; level of business activity, 107; local firm advantages, 3; networks, 98; relocation, 4, 14, 49; risk reduction, 18. *See also* Multi-

193